Consumer's Guide to Alternative Therapies in the Horse

Consumer's Guide to Alternative Therapies in the Horse

by David Ramey, D.V.M.

Howell Book House
New York

Howell Book House
IDG Books Worldwide, Inc.
An International Data Group Company
919 E. Hillsdale Boulevard
Suite 400
Foster City, CA 94404

Howell Book House is a registered trademark of Macmillan General
Reference, USA, Inc., a wholly owned subsidiary of IDG Books
Worldwide, Inc.

 The IDG Books Worldwide logo is a registered trademark
under exclusive license to IDG Books Worldwide, Inc.,
from International Data Group, Inc.

ISBN 1-58245-062-5

Manufactured in the United States of America

10 9 8 7 6 5 4 3 2 1

Book Design: George McKeon
Cover Design: Mike Rutkowski

Dedication

To Jackson and Aidan, may you learn to distinguish between sense and nonsense.

Finding the occasional straw of truth awash in a great ocean of confusion and bam-boozle requires vigilance, dedication and courage. But if we don't practice these tough habits of thought, we cannot hope to solve the true serious problems that face us, and we risk becoming a world of suckers up for grabs by the next charlatan who saunters along.

Carl Sagan,
The Demon Haunted World:
Science as a Candle in the Dark, 1996, p. 38.

Dedication

To Jackson and Aidan, may you learn to distinguish between sense and nonsense.

Finding the occasional straw of truth awash in a great ocean of confusion and bamboozle requires vigilance, dedication and courage. But if we don't practice these tough habits of thought, we cannot hope to solve the true serious problems that face us, and we risk becoming a world of suckers up for grabs by the next charlatan who saunters along.

Carl Sagan,
The Demon Haunted World:
Science as a Candle in the Dark, 1996, p. 38.

Acknowledgments

This book could not have been written without the considerable help and accumulated expertise of the many experts who were consulted in each field. The author wanted to make sure that the information provided in this book was as up-to-date and thorough as possible. The various experts (who are also acknowledged in each chapter) made sure that goal was achieved. That such a prestigious and accomplished group was willing to so generously give of their time and expertise to this project is truly humbling.

Without the efforts of Madelyn Larsen, this book would never have been written. The subject matter herein is that of controversy; controversy is not always a field in which the media wants to play. Her patience and support made not only this book, but a whole series of books, come to life.

Jennifer Bryant, horseowner and freelance editor, was terrific in helping me make sure that my goal of providing not only good, but also understandable, information was attained. Bob Imrie, D.V.M., of Seattle, is a constant source of encouragement and support. He shares the same concerns on the small animal side of veterinary medicine and the same hope that something good may eventually come of all this. The readers of the book who freely give their time always find areas that could be more clear. This time, Jonna Pangburn Dennis sends her artistic take from Texas, Anja Zimmermann's comments come from Munich and Linda Rarey's insights come from California.

Finally, to my wife Elizabeth, the seeker of run-on sentences, thanks for your support. Between work and the boys (Jackson and Aidan), you perform quite a feat.

Contents

Introduction

There are only two types of medicine: that which works and that which does not. The trick is in trying to find out which is which.

When I graduated from veterinary school, I recited an oath with my graduating classmates. I solemnly swore to "use my scientific knowledge and skills for the benefit of society through the protection of animal health, the relief of animal suffering, the conservation of livestock resources, the promotion of public health and the advancement of medical knowledge." I promised I would "practice my profession conscientiously, with dignity and in keeping with the principles of veterinary medical ethics." And I accepted "as a lifelong obligation the continual improvement of my professional knowledge and competence." I took that oath seriously.

I graduated from veterinary school in 1983. Since that time, I've seen any number of therapies come and go. The current rage is a variety of unrelated treatments that go by such names as *alternative*, *complementary*, and *integrative*. I didn't learn about any of them in veterinary school.

Over time, my clients began to ask me about alternative therapies. I really didn't know what to say. It didn't seem right for me to tell people to try some therapy on their horses about which I knew nothing. Nor did it seem right for me to tell people that they *shouldn't* try some therapy, just because I didn't know anything about it. That's where my oath came in: It meant that I had an obligation to look into these so-called alternative therapies to find out whether there was something else out there that I could use to help horses.

For several years, I've studied subjects such as manual therapy, homeopathy, acupuncture, herbal therapy and nutraceuticals in medical-school libraries. I've consulted with experts in various fields. I learned that the veterinary community has not yet conducted good, thorough investigations of the utility of alternative therapies. From that discovery was born the idea for this book: to offer the equine community some perspective amidst the hype.

Horse owners today are bombarded with books, magazine articles and even television shows about their animals' health and the purported benefits of alternative therapies. But if you lack a scientific or medical background, you may be unable to figure out if what you are being told is the truth. For example, you may understand that *arthritis* refers to the breakdown of a joint. But do you know the cellular structure of joint cartilage? Do you understand the chemical events that occur within an arthritic joint? If you don't, can you assess the claims made by nutraceutical manufacturers? The answer is yes—if you know how to look for and evaluate the evidence.

The best way to look for evidence is to use the tools of science. The scientific method is the most important tool ever developed for gaining knowledge. The systems of science and medicine have been responsible for some of the most significant discoveries in human history. From antibiotics to aspirin, science and medicine have worked hand in hand to advance the treatment of disease. At one time, medicine was more magic and superstition than science and investigation. Doctors often were viewed—correctly—as doing more harm than good. Leeches and bleedings, purging and cupping all are medical treatments that have been abandoned, at least in part because they failed to stand up to scientific scrutiny.

Science does not and cannot have all the answers, but it is the best known way of formulating and evaluating medical questions. Science doesn't choose sides; it's merely a method of making sure that the observations people make are good ones. It's a way of making sure that people don't fool themselves.

Not everyone agrees that science is a search for the truth. Some say that science is an ideology, that it tries to reduce everything to bits of matter that interact with one another. They believe that science treats living beings like machines and strips life of its dignity and mystery. These people propose alternatives to the systems of science and medicine.

Alternative views suggest that a more *organic, holistic,* or *integrated* approach is appropriate—even though those terms are not easily defined. As such, "alternative" medical practices, may be offered as a way of helping you to care for your horse. They may be promoted as a way to keep your normal horse healthy. In fact, alternative views may be correct. However, the only way to find out whether they are correct is to see whether there is any good evidence for them, and the best way to evaluate evidence is to be scientific about it.

The information and conclusions presented in this book are not the idle musings of a lone veterinarian. A wide variety of experts from the medical and veterinary fields—from M.D.'s to Ph.D.'s, physicists to nutritionists, and philosophers to psychologists—were generous and open with their time and knowledge. The ideas and expertise in this book were initially theirs; to the extent that some of it rubbed off on me, I'm terrifically lucky. The experts helped draft their chapters and reviewed the content for scientific accuracy. As a result, the conclusions presented must be taken seriously by anyone who considers or promotes alternative therapies for horses.

David Ramey, D.V.M.
Chatsworth, California
April 1999

CHAPTER ONE

Why Treatments May Seem to Work (Even When They Don't)

with Barry Beyerstein, Ph.D.

How do you know if a treatment your horse received works? False claims and assumptions of effectiveness abound, whether the treatment is considered scientific medicine, an old folk remedy, an alternative or complementary therapy or a faith healer's hocus-pocus. Many dubious treatment methods remain on the market purely because of the testimonials of satisfied customers. What they're saying is: "I tried it; my horse got better; it works!" The problem is that the horse's improvement doesn't prove that the therapy was responsible.

Providers of treatments and therapies for animals have a professional and ethical obligation to prove, first, that their products and services are safe and second, that they are effective. Demonstrating that a therapy doesn't harm the animal usually is no big deal to do, but proving that the therapy is effective can be quite another matter. Establishing proof is difficult, at least in part, because even honest and intelligent people can be led in subtle ways to believe that a treatment was effective when in fact it was not—and this holds true for both the practitioner and the client.[1]

To evaluate a treatment's effectiveness objectively, you have to be able to establish a direct cause-and-effect relationship between the treatment and the subsequent improvement. Just because the condition improved following treatment, you can't assume that the treatment caused the improvement. Mistaking a *correlation* ("My horse got better after treatment") for a *causation* ("The treatment caused the improvement") is a basic fallacy of logic known as *post hoc, ergo propter hoc* ("It happened *after,* so it was caused *by*").

People have a tendency to assume that, when events occur in sequence, they must be connected. But this is not necessarily true. For example, many people who drink diet soft drinks are overweight. The salaries of preachers have gone up and so has beer consumption. So is it correct to conclude that diet drinks cause obesity or that preachers are using their money to buy more beer? Of course not. But in effect, that's the logic used when people use only their personal experience as the sole method of evaluating a therapy's effectiveness. That's why good research studies use the scientific method, with a control group of subjects who aren't given the drug or treatment in question, to determine whether their condition would have improved without the drug or treatment. Without such controls, you can never know whether things would have gone just as well with no treatment at all.

The question then becomes, "Why might caregivers and their clients, who rely on anecdotal evidence and uncontrolled observations, erroneously conclude that the therapies that they dispense and receive work when they may not?" There are several good reasons.

THE NATURAL COURSE OF DISEASE

"Time heals all wounds." Provided that a condition is not chronic or fatal, the natural tendency of a living organism (like a horse) is to heal itself. Most ailments improve on their own, with or without therapy. Therefore, before you can say that a therapy works, you must show that more patients got better with therapy than would have improved without it or that they improved faster than if they were left alone. Unless you can evaluate the success and failure records of a sufficient number of patients with the same complaint, you can't prove (and shouldn't say) that a particular treatment is more beneficial than leaving the condition alone.

BODY, HEAL THYSELF

How many cases of acute disease improve on their own? You may be astonished at the answer. Depending on which estimates you read, as many as 70 to 90 percent of acute diseases heal without any intervention whatsoever. Those odds mean that as long as the therapy you choose doesn't do any harm, there's a good chance that it will be perceived as successful. On the other hand, of course, many chronic diseases won't get better, no matter how you treat them.

CYCLICAL DISEASES

Conditions such as arthritis, allergies, and gastrointestinal problems have ups and downs. The symptoms may be lessened on some days and worse on others. Most people seek treatment for their horses during the downturns, when things are the worst. In this way, treatments may coincide with upturns that might happen anyway. Without valid controlled studies, it's easy to misinterpret improvement from a normal cyclical variation as a valid therapeutic effect.

THE PLACEBO EFFECT

Strange but true: When people are given a treatment that's inactive, they sometimes feel better. This phenomenon is known as the *placebo effect*. In humans, the placebo effect is not necessarily all in the mind; the body can show improvement, too. The reasons for this aren't clear, but some experts say it largely depends on the power of suggestion.

It would stand to reason that animals can't demonstrate the placebo effect, because they don't know what treatment they're getting. But their owners do! Recent research indicates that up to 70 percent of past medical or surgical patients reported good results from techniques known today to be ineffective—perhaps because, at the time of the treatment, the patient and the doctor believed the treatment to be effective.[2] Some crackpot procedures (by today's standards) were once enthusiastically endorsed by physicians and patients alike.[3] So it's entirely reasonable to suspect that, if a horse owner trusts a practitioner and a therapy method, he or

4

she will report improvement, especially in nebulous categories such as "better performance," "improved disposition," and "increased healing."

To distinguish placebo effects from specific changes in the disease process resulting from a given treatment, tests must be conducted in which patients are randomly assigned to groups and the patients (or their owners) are "blind" to whether they're receiving a placebo or the real thing. The evaluators also should be "blind" as to which patients are receiving treatment—hence the term *double blind*, which is the gold standard of scientific research.

PSYCHOSOMATIC PROBLEMS

A horse owner who believes that his or her otherwise healthy animal is performing poorly may suspect some undefined physical problem. A practitioner may offer the owner welcome reassurance and support, which may even be enough to take care of the problem (for the owner, anyway). However, providing emotional support and reassurance to a concerned horse owner is not necessarily medical or scientific.

The downside of catering to the desire for medical diagnoses for vague complaints is that it opens the door for any number of poorly defined diagnoses that cannot be demonstrated by reproducible methods. That's bad because it means that there's no way to verify them. It also provides unlimited opportunities for medical quacks, who are often aided by the use of pseudoscientific devices and treatments to which "success" is then attributed.

SYMPTOMATIC RELIEF VERSUS CURE

Short of coming up with a cure, most horse owners want to ensure that their animals are not in pain or discomfort. Research indicates that humans' perception of pain is part sensation (the physical feeling) and part emotion. If the emotional component can be controlled, people may feel better, even if the underlying physiological basis of the pain remains.

How does this relate to horses? Horse owners want to make sure their animals aren't suffering. Anything that can allay their anxiety, redirect their attention, foster a sense of control over their problems, or lead to a reinterpretation of the signs of pain can help them cope with the problem. Human pain clinics use such symptomatic strategies every day.[4] If you perceive that your horse suffers less as a result of a treatment, that's great; but don't confuse a symptomatic treatment with a bona fide cure.

THE POWER OF POSITIVE THINKING

Providers and receivers of therapy alike may be remarkably confident that a therapy works, even when it doesn't. A 1993 study evaluated five therapies, both surgical and medical, that are now known to be ineffective. Amazingly, at the time they were provided, approximately 70 percent of both the doctors and the patients were convinced that the therapies worked. That's some testimony to the power of self-persuasion.

HEDGING YOUR BETS

Many horses receive more than one treatment at a time, so one treatment or another may receive a disproportionate share of the credit for the improvement. When alternative or complementary treatments are combined with scientific therapies, credit may be given where credit isn't due.

MISDIAGNOSIS

Some horse owners fear that their animals are suffering from conditions they clearly don't have. Take the well-publicized and relatively recent concern about equine protozoal myelitis (EPM), for example. Some owners appear ready to ascribe any vague sign of decreased performance or minor, intermittent gait problem (such as the occasional stumble) to EPM, a serious disease. Considering the apparent large incidence of exposure and the relative difficulty of obtaining an accurate diagnosis (EPM cannot be diagnosed merely by drawing blood, and even spinal-fluid analysis can lead to a false positive diagnosis), many horses that are treated for EPM clearly don't have it.

Of course, conventional diagnostic techniques are not infallible. A misdiagnosis followed by an alternative treatment may lead to a glowing account of a miraculous cure for a grave condition that never existed. Furthermore, if conventional veterinarians fail to come up with a plausible cause of the perceived problem, the owner may gravitate toward alternative practitioners, who can

7

almost always find some sort of imbalance to treat. (If "recovery" follows, another alternative-therapy convert is born.)

DISTORTION OF REALITY

Even when a treatment produces no improvement whatsoever, people who have a strong psychological investment in the therapy can convince themselves that improvement has occurred.[5] According to a psychological theory known as *cognitive dissonance*, [6] when experiences contradict existing attitudes, feelings, or knowledge, mental distress is produced. People tend to resolve this conflict by reinterpreting (distorting) the offending information. In the case of alternative therapies, a horse owner may experience such a conflict when he or she sees no improvement after investing time, energy, and money in a treatment. Instead of admitting that the treatment was a waste of time and money, that person may will him- or herself to find some redeeming value in the treatment.

Other *self-serving biases* can help to defend strong beliefs in the face of contradictory evidence.[7] Practitioners and clients tend to remember things as they wish they had happened. They may be selective in what they remember, overestimating successes while ignoring, downplaying, or explaining away failures.

An illusory feeling that things have gotten better also may result from the therapeutic setting's *demand characteristics*. People generally feel obligated to reciprocate when somebody does them a good deed. Most therapists sincerely believe that they are helping their patients, and it is only natural that their clients want to please them in return. These feelings of obligation or *compliance effects*—however unconscious they may be—may be enough to inflate a client's perception of a treatment's effectiveness.[8]

Individual testimonies of a treatment's effectiveness, though often compelling, actually should count for very little in your overall evaluation of that treatment. The proof should be in the form of results of scientific tests that control for placebo responses, compliance effects and judgmental errors. Any therapy that is supported only by testimonials, self-published books and pamphlets or media coverage should immediately be considered suspect. Even a single positive outcome from a carefully controlled experiment can be a fluke. If a practitioner of any therapy claims to be persecuted, is openly hostile to mainstream science, can't supply a concrete reason for the therapy's effectiveness that agrees with known principles or promises incredible results, there is good reason to be suspicious of that practitioner.

THE TROUBLE WITH TESTIMONY

In 1988, the National Research Council expressed its views on personal testimony:

People are typically weak at identifying the range of [possible causes of positive change in their lives], however simply they may be described, and at distinguishing the different ways in which the causal forces might operate. How can people know how they would have matured over time in the absence of an intervention (technique) that is being assessed? How can people disentangle effects due to a pleasant experience, a dynamic leader, or a sense of doing something important from effects due to the critical components of the treatment per se? Much research has shown that individuals are poor intuitive scientists and that they recreate a set of known cognitive biases. These include belief perseverance, selective memory, errors in attribution and overconfidence. These biases influence experts and non-experts alike, usually without one's awareness of them.

If you believe that your horse is unwell, it's only natural that you want to try anything that holds a promise of a cure. The problem is that false hopes may supersede your common sense. It's when you're most desperate and vulnerable that you need to be most aware and analytical—and that's not an easy thing to do.

BARRY BEYERSTEIN

Barry Beyerstein, Ph.D., is an associate professor of psychology and a member of the Brain Behavior Laboratory at Simon Fraser University in Vancouver, British Columbia, Canada. He holds a bachelor's degree from Simon Fraser University and a Ph.D. in experimental and biological psychology from the University of California at Berkeley. He has studied the brain mechanisms of perception and consciousness and the effects of drugs on the brain and mind. He has investigated the scientific status of many questionable products in the areas of medical and psychological treatment, as well as a number of dubious self-improvement techniques. He has become an expert in the psychology of human error—how failures of memory and inference and psychological processes such

10

as self-deception and wishful thinking can lead to false but comforting beliefs about the world.

Dr. Beyerstein is a Fellow and a member of the Executive Council of the Committee for the Scientific Investigation of Claims of the Paranormal and is on the editorial board of its journal, *The Skeptical Inquirer*. He is an elected member of the Council for Scientific Medicine and a contributing editor to the *Scientific Review of Alternative Medicine*.

NOTES

1. Beyerstein, B. "Why Bogus Therapies Seem to Work." *Skeptical Inquirer* 27(5) (1997): 29–34.

2. Roberts, A. H., et al. "The Power of Nonspecific Effects in Healing: Implications for Psychological and Biological Treatments." *Clinical Psychology Review* 13 (1993): 375–391.

3. Barrett, S., and Jarvis, W. *The Health Robbers: A Close Look at Quackery in America*. Amherst, NY: Prometheus Books, 1993.

4. Smith, W., Merskey, H., and Gross, S., editors. *Pain: Meaning and Management*. New York: SP Medical & Scientific Books, 1980.

5. Alcock, J. "The Belief Engine." *Skeptical Inquirer* 19(3)(1995): 14–18.

6. Festinger, L. *A Theory of Cognitive Dissonance*. Palo Alto, CA: Stanford University Press, 1957.

7. Beyerstein, G., and Hadaway, P. "On Avoiding Folly." *Journal of Drug Issues* 20(4) (1991): 689–700.

8. Adair, J. *The Human Subject*. Boston: Little, Brown, 1973.

as self-deception and wishful thinking can lead to false but comforting beliefs about the world.

Dr. Beyerstein is a Fellow and a member of the Executive Council of the Committee for the Scientific Investigation of Claims of the Paranormal and is on the editorial board of its journal, *The Skeptical Inquirer*. He is an elected member of the Council for Scientific Medicine and a contributing editor to the *Scientific Review of Alternative Medicine*.

NOTES

1. Beyerstein, B. "Why Bogus Therapies Seem to Work." *Skeptical Inquirer* 27(5) (1997): 29–34.

2. Roberts, A. H., et al. "The Power of Nonspecific Effects in Healing: Implications for Psychological and Biological Treatments." *Clinical Psychology Review* 13 (1993): 375–391.

3. Barrett, S., and Jarvis, W. *The Health Robbers: A Close Look at Quackery in America*. Amherst, NY: Prometheus Books, 1993.

4. Smith, W., Merskey, H., and Gross, S., editors. *Pain: Meaning and Management*. New York: SP Medical & Scientific Books, 1980.

5. Alcock, J. "The Belief Engine." *Skeptical Inquirer* 19(3)(1995): 14–18.

6. Festinger, L. *A Theory of Cognitive Dissonance*. Palo Alto, CA: Stanford University Press, 1957.

7. Beyerstein, G., and Hadaway, P. "On Avoiding Folly." *Journal of Drug Issues* 20(4) (1991): 689–700.

8. Adair, J. *The Human Subject*. Boston: Little, Brown, 1973.

Chapter Two

How to Evaluate Evidence That Things Work

with *Lewis Vaughn*

Just because a therapy's claims are a bit odd doesn't necessarily mean they aren't true. For example, it is entirely possible that homeopathic remedies (discussed in Chapter 12) are effective in treating a variety of equine medical problems. The question you need to answer in evaluating whether any therapy works is "How do I know it's working?" It's a question of *epistemology*, which is the study of how you know what you know.

Here are some of the most common rationales offered in support of various therapies:

1. You tried it, and it worked.

2. Somebody else tried it, and it worked.

3. A medical expert says it works.

4. A medical expert's observations of several patients show that it works.

5. It's been around for a long time, and many people have used it.

6. A scientific study shows that it works.

Each of these reasons needs to be examined more thoroughly so you know what weight to give it.

PERSONAL EXPERIENCE

You're concerned that your horse isn't jumping to his full potential. You have an equine chiropractor adjust him, and his jumping improves. What could be more natural than to credit the chiropractic treatment for that result? Shouldn't your own experience be the best, most direct indication of whether treatment works?

Many people think so. In fact, many claims made for alternative therapies are based completely on such testimonial evidence of effectiveness. For example, why would a friend tell you that a treatment worked if he or she weren't convinced that it had? However, personal experience alone doesn't constitute proof of a treatment's effectiveness. As you learned in Chapter I, there are many reasons that a treatment may seem to work when it really doesn't.

It's important to remember that, just as one person's experience generally can't demonstrate that a therapy is effective, neither can the experience of many people. Lots of people believe that vitamin C helps prevent colds; scientific research has shown that it doesn't. If one piece of unreliable evidence isn't good, more pieces of unreliable evidence aren't any better. The testimonial evidence offered by satisfied users or practitioners of a therapy generally doesn't prove much of anything—except, perhaps, that some people have strong beliefs about certain treatments. Belief is not evidence. Unfortunately, most people aren't very good at identifying the range of possible causes of the events in their lives.

EXPERT ENDORSEMENT

One veterinarian says that a certain homeopathic remedy cures colic. Another vet tells you that using a laser will speed the healing of your horse's tendon injury. Are these statements true just because they were made by veterinarians? After all, aren't veterinarians legitimate authorities?

THE LITTLE SURGERY THAT COULDN'T

In the 1950s, some doctors thought they had discovered a cure for angina pectoris, a painful heart condition: Surgeons would tie off a chest artery in an attempt to improve blood flow to the heart. Most of the patients on whom the surgery was performed reported dramatic improvement in their condition. Later controlled studies, in which some patients received a phony surgery, showed that both treated and untreated subjects experienced relief of their symptoms. The procedure was soon abandoned.

You rely on your veterinarian to give you accurate information about your horse's health and to make him better when he's sick, injured or unsound. Unfortunately, though, the information you're given isn't always accurate; in fact, the two claims mentioned, both of which have been made by veterinarians, are unproven at best and untrue at worst. How can this happen?

An authority's endorsement may be a good reason to believe a claim if that authority is qualified to speak on the issue. Veterinarians are authorities in the diagnosis of disease and in the art of apply-ing healing techniques and technology to their patients. They should have the know-how to treat horse diseases. However, they may not be authorities on which remedies work and don't work. For example, although a qualified veterinarian should be able to recog-nize an injury to a limb, he or she may not be an expert in the physics of magnetic fields, a realm of alternative therapy that advocates say helps heal such injuries.

The problem is further compounded if the "authoritative" in-formation comes from a false authority, a person who sounds very knowledgeable about a subject but who may lack training in medical techniques and diagnosis. The world of equine medicine appears to be filled with people with no relevant educational back-ground who are diagnosing conditions and providing therapies.

Veterinarians may be tempted to rely solely on their own ex-periences from working with animals and talking to horse owners as evidence for various therapies' effectiveness. But a medical provider's personal experiences are as potentially unreliable as those of the patient or client. A veterinarian's work with horses generally cannot produce the evidence required for him or her to decide whether a therapy really works.

"OK," you may reason, "why can't a veterinarian administer a treatment to several horses with the same problem, keep records of the reactions and then draw valid conclusions about the treatment's effectiveness?" The answer: such studies, called *case reports*, are sub-ject to the same limitations that apply to personal experience. It's easy to overlook the variable nature of diseases, placebo effects and other factors that can impair the veterinarian's ability to draw a valid conclusion about whether a treatment works. Even if he or she keeps extensive records, case studies aren't subjected to the strict controls found in scientific studies. Without controls, other factors can't be ruled out.

To illustrate, suppose your horse is diagnosed with a sore back. Acupuncture is suggested as a treatment, and he seems better afterward. Would his condition have improved anyway, with or without the acupuncture? Or did he not really improve at all, and you just think he did? Did you change saddles or exercise regimens while he was receiving the treatment? Did he receive another kind of treatment at the same time? Case reports usually don't answer these kinds of questions.

Case reports also are vulnerable to two serious biases that confound results. One of these biases is called *social desirability.* Most people want to respond to treatment in what they perceive is the correct way. As a result, they may report improvement because they think they should or because they want to please the doctor.

The second bias, called *investigational bias,* can come from the doctors themselves. People who are investigating a treatment sometimes see an effect in a patient because they want or expect to see it. For example, a chiropractor's investment in the results or anticipation of how subjects are likely to respond can easily become a self-fulfilling prophecy—not because the chiropractor is dishonest, but because it's tough to be objective when you're hoping to see good results.

Based on the limitations of personal experience and case studies, you can reasonably state: *When a treatment's claims of effectiveness are based solely on personal experience or case studies, you generally cannot know whether the treatment is effective.*

IS RUDOLPH REAL?

Here's a hypothesis: Rudolph the Red-Nosed Reindeer is real and lives at the North Pole. What's the evidence? Millions of people (albeit mostly children) believe him to be real; his likeness appears regularly during the Christmas holidays; there are many reindeer in the world, and it's possible that through normal genetic variations a reindeer that flies could have evolved; some people say that they have seen Rudolph with their own eyes. Are you convinced?

THE APPEAL TO TRADITION

Have you ever heard this commonly submitted claim of effectiveness? "Because this therapy has been around for thousands of years, we know that it works." Of course you have. But just because something has been around for a long time doesn't mean it's legitimate. Take astrology, for one—an ersatz and thoroughly discredited science that's been around for more than 2,000 years. Or what about the ancient African tribal practice of eating the heart of a lion to assimilate the animal's spirit?

The point here is not to pooh-pooh therapies with roots in ancient folk practices. Some of them may have a legitimate basis; take the use of pharmacological substances that are derived from plants, for example. The point is that the mere fact that a treatment has been around for a long time isn't proof that it's effective.

18

BLINDED BY SCIENCE

Just as you've heard the appeal to tradition, you've probably also heard this statement: "Scientific studies show that treatment ABC is effective." This statement certainly sounds convincing, and it's true that scientific evidence obtained through controlled experimentation eventually can establish beyond a reasonable doubt whether a treatment works.

Unfortunately, practically every practitioner and manufacturer cites scientific findings to support their services and products. Some assessments of scientific information are reliable and informative; others are biased, worthless and/or misleading. But if you're not a scientist, how are you supposed to sort out appeals to science? You can begin by learning some of the characteristics and limitations of scientific evidence.

Scientific studies (also called experiments) are the basic mechanisms of scientific research. They can be done on cells in a test tube or on horses (or other animals) themselves. Researchers use studies to evaluate their hypotheses of how things may work. Good scientific studies are performed under carefully controlled conditions that are intended to help ensure that the observations made are as objective and accurate as possible. The results of a good scientific study can provide evidence for or fail to support a particular hypothesis.

After a study is completed, the researcher tries to get it published in a scientific journal. The best journals subject those studies to *peer review*; that is, other experts in the field examine the study to see whether it should be accepted, modified or rejected. After the study is published, other researchers can examine it, criticize it or try to reproduce the results themselves (replication of studies is a critical step in confirming whether they are true). In this way, science progresses. Behind this tidy picture, however, are some untidy facts of which you should be aware.

SINGLE STUDIES

The results of a single study generally cannot establish that a treatment works. Good medical research is a tedious process, and many things can go wrong. Several scientific reviews of human medical studies have concluded that a large percentage of published studies are seriously flawed: The number of individuals studied may have been too small to produce valid results; the statistical analysis of the data may have been flawed; in rare cases, the data may even have been faked. That's why it's important that studies be repeated by independent investigators. The chances that multiple studies that produce identical results are all flawed are small.

CONFLICTING RESULTS

Sometimes, studies show conflicting results. Errors that occur in one study can lead to results that conflict with an identical yet error-free study. The results of preliminary studies can conflict with the results of more carefully controlled, longer-term trials. When studies conflict, people get confused because they don't know what to conclude. Logic dictates that, if the results of studies conflict, you can't know if the treatment that is being studied works. You can't just go with the study that best supports what you're trying to prove or what you want to believe.

Studies That Conflict with Fact

A study may come along that conflicts with previously established scientific evidence. Suppose that a new study shows that deworming medications cause deadly colic in horses. You wouldn't necessarily accept that study as the truth—and not just because it's a single study. You'd doubt it because mountains of evidence exist that deworming horses is safe and in their best interests. It would be more reasonable to suspect a flaw in the study than to stop relying on the previously established information. If more evidence came along to support the new, revolutionary finding that deworing horses is bad for them, researchers would be forced to rethink the issue and eventually would have to discard the old view in favor of the new.

The different types of medical studies differ dramatically in their strength to support hypotheses about the effectiveness of treatments or of cause-and-effect relationships. If you're trying to make sense of clinical research, you need to understand the differences and give more credence to the stronger types of studies.

Test-tube Studies

Test-tube studies (which may not actually be conducted in test tubes but are not conducted on living animals or people) are called *in vitro* studies. They can offer some weak evidence to support a hypothesis or provide clues about how something might work; the drawback is that what happens in a test tube or a petri dish may never happen in an animal's body. The effects of a substance that works well in a test tube can't be extrapolated directly to the horse because any number of bodily functions or processes may block, dilute or change its effect. Therefore, test-tube studies cannot establish a treatment's effectiveness.

STUDIES ON OTHER ANIMALS

Studies performed on one species can help researchers understand diseases in other species. However, each species has a different genetic and physiologic makeup. For example, a single, effective dose of xylazine, a tranquilizer commonly used in horses, is ten times as effective in a cow but only one-tenth as effective in a pig. Because of interspecies differences, studies on one species cannot generally establish whether a treatment works in another species.

OBSERVATIONAL STUDIES

Observational studies of groups of horses are also known as non-intervention or epidemiological studies. These studies include several types, with names such as retrospective, prospective, case-control, cohort and cross-sectional. None of these types involves hands-on or invasive testing; instead, these studies are used to look for associations among various health-related factors and disease. Such a study might reveal, say, an association between horses' exercise levels and the incidence of catastrophic limb injuries.

The important thing to remember is that observational studies alone cannot prove cause-and-effect relationships; they can only show associations and hint at possible causes. For example, the study of equine exercise levels and limb injuries couldn't prove that exercise causes horses to get catastrophic injuries; it could show only that one factor (exercise) is linked to a problem (injuries).

All sorts of associations can be found in such studies. For example, children today watch more television than in days past; they're also taller. Does that mean that watching television promotes growth in children? Remember, just because one thing follows another, it doesn't necessarily mean that the first thing caused the second.

CLINICAL TRIALS

Of all of the types of medical studies, clinical trials offer the strongest and best support for a treatment's claims of effectiveness, because they *can* establish cause and effect beyond a reasonable doubt. Clinical trials allow researchers to control variables that can affect treatment and to test one factor at a time.

In clinical trials intended to test treatments' effectiveness, one group receives the treatment in question while a second group, which is as similar as possible to the first, does not. The second group is called the *control group*. Researchers then compare differences between the two groups to verify whether the treatment had any effect.

The use of a control group is vital; without it, there's no way of knowing whether the treatment worked. In some studies, control-group members receive placebos; if the treatment is effective, it should perform much better than the placebo.

Another important element of a clinical trial is *blinding*, which prevents both the subjects and the researchers from having knowledge of the experiment that could taint the results. Well-designed clinical trials are *double-blind*, in which neither the subjects nor the examiners know who's getting what.

Even clinical trials can lead to faulty conclusions. At least three clinical trial defects can easily be detected by nonscientists:

1. *Lack of a control group.* Without a control group, a clinical trial proves little or nothing. Evidence from noncontrolled clinical trials is about as useful as evidence from testimonials and case studies.

2. *Faulty comparisons.* In clinical trials, the control group and the group getting the treatment should be comparable. Horses used in studies should be of the same sex, age group, and general health status, for example. To protect against using noncomparable groups, scientists use a technique called *randomization,* in which subjects are assigned randomly to either control or experimental groups. Randomization helps to ensure that any differences among subjects are evenly distributed. Lack of randomization can be a pivotal defect in a study.

3. *Small numbers.* Clinical trials with fewer than 30 subjects are generally suspect. With such small numbers, the chance increases that some confusing variable will occur. Small studies increase the odds that a treatment will appear to work when it actually doesn't. In addition, small studies usually are brief and therefore can't shed light on a treatment's effects on long-lasting or chronic conditions.

Without solid evidence, there is no rational basis for drawing a conclusion about a treatment's effectiveness. You're forced to rely on your beliefs alone. Beliefs may be powerful motivators, but they are not a legitimate basis for making decisions that affect your horse's health.

LEWIS VAUGHN

Lewis Vaughn is executive editor of the *Scientific Review of Alternative Medicine.* With co-author Theodore Schick, Ph.D., he has written two college textbooks, *How to Think About Weird Things* and *Doing Philosophy.*

CHAPTER THREE

Scientific Versus Unscientific Thinking

with William T. Jarvis, Ph.D.

Anyone can use the scientific process to arrive at and advance his or her beliefs. At the same time, anyone—no matter how scientific—can wander off the scientific path. A scientist is not a special class of person; rather, "scientist" is a label that anyone who acts scientifically can earn. The uniqueness of science is found in the way that scientists acquire knowledge, remain objective about their beliefs, and advance their beliefs.

The scientific language is littered with words that reflect mistaken ideas. In 1657, the English physician Thomas Willis named a disease for his belief that its sudden appearance was caused by the stars' evil influence: influenza (the flu). Another disease, malaria, was believed to be caused by bad air (*mala aria* in Italian). *Vitamin* is a contraction of the words *vital* and *amine* and was coined by a scientist who thought he had found the primary food necessary for life (what he had discovered was vitamin B_1, also known as thiamine).

Scientific knowledge doesn't just happen; it's hard work. It's also contrary to human nature. People believe more than they know, for cannot possibly know all that they believe. People with a scientific mindset readily admit that some questions have not been answered and are comfortable with that fact. People who aren't content with unanswered questions may try to fill the gaps with beliefs.

An early demonstration of the usefulness of scientific investigations revealed the power of human imagination as a source of clinical illusions. In eighteenth-century France, patients and practitioners said they could sense feelings of discomfort or heat coming from objects that had been "magnetized." In an experiment led by none other than Benjamin Franklin, a twelve-year-old boy who believed himself sensitive to magnetism was blindfolded and led to four trees that, unbeknownst to him, had not been "magnetized." After embracing each tree for two minutes, the boy reacted dramatically and claimed he felt strong symptoms. Through this and other tests, it became obvious to the Franklin Commission that the believers had active imaginations but not "animal magnetism."

REACTIVE EFFECTS

Like the tree-hugging boy, recipients of alternative therapies (or their owners) may respond in ways that are unrelated to the treatments. In other words, a horse owner may perceive improvement in her animal when no improvement has taken place. Such responses are known as *reactive effects,* and some are so well-known that they have specific names.

THE HAWTHORNE EFFECT

The Hawthorne effect is named for a series of behavioral experiments at Western Electric's plant in Hawthorne, Illinois. No matter what the researchers did, the workers' performance reportedly improved, allegedly because they knew they were being observed (although re-examination of the original data has cast doubt on the fact that performance *always* improved).

THE ROSENTHAL EFFECT

People like to please those whom they like or respect. People who receive medical treatment tend to give the therapist what they think the therapist wants to see. Similarly, if you take your horse to a famous veterinary clinic, you might be inclined to see a favorable response for a while.

OBSERVER BIAS

If you want to see something badly enough, you probably will see it, whether it is there or not. This tendency is one of the failings of human perception that must be circumvented through the use of scientific methodology.

THE CASE OF CLEVER HANS

In 1904, a retired German schoolteacher, Wilhelm von Osten, claimed that his horse, who came to be known as Clever Hans, could answer arithmetic problems, tell time, and recognize photographs of people that he had met, among other things. Clever Hans would answer the questions put to him by tapping his hoof. A panel of German scientists investigated him and concluded that the horse was a genuine phenomenon.

One doubter, Oskar Pfungst, a prominent German psychologist of his day, noted that Hans didn't get the right answer when his audience didn't know the answer. Pfungst concluded that Hans was responding to some sort of unintentional visual cues. He was right: Hans was so sensitive that he reacted to subtle postural changes. If Hans were "counting," for instance, his observers would unconsciously tense their muscles until the horse had pawed the correct number of times. When the audience relaxed, Hans stopped pawing.

THE WAYS OF SCIENCE

In an attempt to overcome the limitations of observation, science builds its findings on a foundation of proof. Here's how it works.

SCIENCE DEFINES, SPECIFIES AND QUANTIFIES. Everybody agrees that good nutrition is important for horses, but not everybody agrees on what constitutes good nutrition. Nutritionists define, specify and quantify it in terms of nutrients, minimum dietary requirements, ideal protein levels and so forth; nonscientists may counter with such terms as *natural, whole foods,* or *improved bloom*—terms that either can't be defined or are meaningless.

SCIENCE SETS LIMITS ON HOW FAR A BELIEF CAN BE CARRIED OR APPLIED. Good nutrition is important for your horse, sure, but will it prevent colic, arthritis or the effects of aging? Scientifically valid therapies are tested for clinical value, safety and effectiveness in treating specific conditions. One of the failings of unscientific medicine is that its developers and practitioners may be unwilling to place clear limitations on what a therapy can and cannot treat. (Can acupuncture, for example, really help *every* condition, as some proponents claim?)

SCIENCE EXPLAINS HOW THINGS WORK. Once you understand how something works, it can be more precisely applied. Of course, sometimes you don't care *how* a medicine or a treatment works, as long as it works. People knew that aspirin worked for more than seventy years before they ever figured out how it worked. Still, plenty of good evidence existed to prove aspirin's effectiveness before scientists got around to figuring out precisely how it works.

SCIENCE DELIBERATELY SUBJECTS ITSELF TO SYSTEMATIC SCRUTINY. It's what you think you already know that keeps you from learning. People tend to see what they believe and believe what they see, a process called *selective affirmation*. They focus on the positive findings that reinforce their convictions while ignoring or explaining away contradictory outcomes. Science tries to overcome the selective affirmation bias by trying to prove itself wrong, unearthing new and better information in the process. Because natural perceptions can deceive even the most well-intended observer, scientists make special efforts to try to prove that their ideas *don't* work.

USE OF SCIENTIFIC METHODS. Scientists clearly define their terms. They develop and test their theories under strict conditions. They subject their work to peer review and publish their findings for everyone to see and study.

SCIENCE VERSUS UNSCIENTIFIC THINKING: SIMILARITIES

Scientific and unscientific thinking share many similarities, which is why it can be so difficult to tell them apart.

CREATIVITY AND INTUITION. Artists and inventors, scientists and quacks, geniuses and madmen—all can be creative and intuitive. Both creativity and insanity are departures from common and traditional ways of thinking, and both can lead to new and unique perspectives. But there is one big difference: A creative idea has a basis in reality, even if there isn't enough evidence to convince others of its validity; an insane idea is rooted in internal stimulation: hallucinations, imagined events or speculation.

No one is suggesting that unscientific thinking is necessarily insane; we're merely saying that it's based on imagination, not good evidence. In the case of alternative therapies, this means that responsible veterinary professionals will be cautious in applying imaginative ideas that aren't backed by solid evidence.

THEORIES TO EXPLAIN MECHANISMS OF ACTION. Anyone who uses a treatment wants it to make sense. Both scientists and unscientific thinkers advance theories to explain why their therapies work.

DATA GATHERING. Scientists and nonscientists alike gather information that relates to their theories, methods, and procedures. The data gathered tends to be selective and to confirm the theory being proposed.

NEED FOR CONFIRMING EVIDENCE. Most people won't continue to pursue a course of action that obviously doesn't work. Both scientists and alternative thinkers want to gather evidence that appears to support their hypotheses. Unfortunately, nothing works 100 percent of the time. Through selective data-gathering, even treatments that don't work can be made to appear effective.

COMMITMENT. Great scientists are hard at work in their labs, committed to the next important discovery. Nonscientists can be just as committed, if not downright fanatical in their zeal. The point is that both sides may genuinely care about and may be trying to help your horse, so commitment and concern alone aren't enough to judge a therapist's competence.

SELF-CONFIDENCE. It takes a bulletproof ego to pursue an idea in the face of incomplete evidence. Both scientists and unscientific thinkers may appear confident in their abilities and therapies. Unfortunately, only with hindsight can we judge which confidences were misplaced.

SCIENCE VERSUS UNSCIENTIFIC THINKING: DIFFERENCES

You can evaluate any form of therapy using scientific thinking. Doing so helps you recognize "alternative" ways of thinking that are at odds with science. The following are some indicators of unscientific thinking:

1. Unscientific thinking often calls for an "open mind." But don't confuse open-mindedness with empty-mindedness. Open-minded

31

thinkers are willing to examine new and unusual ideas, but they do so in a critical and objective fashion. Empty-minded thinkers, on the other hand, fail to maintain a healthy skepticism; they can be swayed by perception and their own subjective experience.

Scientific minds, although open, are intolerant. Science doesn't look kindly on ideas that contradict known physical laws, that aren't based on sound reasoning, that are inconsistent with known data or that lack supporting evidence.

2. Unscientific thinking may contain a strong bias against science. It may demand absolute proof of the value of scientific procedures while accepting low-quality evidence to support its own methods. It may accept testimonial evidence as proof.

3. Unscientific thinking is willing to accept a practice or theory as valid merely because it has been around for a while.

4. Unscientific thinking commonly adds a cultural bias to the discussion of therapies. It may pit "Western" and "Eastern" approaches against each other and charge that the differences between science-based medicine and nonstandard practices are merely cultural; asserting one's superiority over another, it may argue, is akin to racism. What such arguments fail to acknowledge is that physical laws, anatomy, physiology, and other scientific disciplines know no cultural bounds.

In truth, Western prescientific cultures differed little from those in the East in their fanciful cosmologies and beliefs. The "vital force" of homeopathy, "animal magnetism" and the "innate" of chiropractic—all arose in the West and are just as mystical as the *qi* of Chinese medicine or the *prana* of ayurvedic practices.

5. Many unscientific thinkers advance unproven or discredited physiological concepts such as cleansing, detoxification and purification of the body.

6. Unscientific thinkers may view criticism of their theories or activities as opposition and efforts to regulate their practices as persecution. They may regard themselves as modern-day innovators whose theories eventually will be confirmed by science.

7. Unscientific thinkers are fond of coming up with theories but refuse to put them to the test. They may call on others to test their ideas, pleading lack of funds. They may claim that "the establishment" is out to stop their advancements because their success would overturn established industries. They may state that they don't need to test their methods because their success is all the evidence they require.

8. Unscientific thinkers may act in ways that oppose the ideas of consumer protection. Any of the following actions is a warning that a therapy provider may not be acting in the best interest of consumers:

   • Failure to disclose the nature of products or procedures used (that is, claims of secret remedies, mysterious devices or miraculous methods).

   • Failure to demonstrate the safety of procedures.

   • Failure to demonstrate the effectiveness of procedures.

   • Failure to follow up to discover unanticipated adverse reactions after products are developed or prescribed.

   • Self-promotion; claims of superiority to other health-care providers.

   • False or misleading advertising (for example, saying "Leading scientists agree" without identifying the scientists).

   • Failure to warn of a treatment's potential adverse effects.

   • Failure to warn of a therapy's limitations.

Unscientific thinking can cloud your good judgment when you need good judgment the most. If your horse is healthy, you can try practically any unscientific thing you want, and it will probably be just fine. But if you treat a serious problem with an unproven therapy, you may end up with a condition more grave than that with which you started.

WILLIAM JARVIS

William Jarvis, Ph.D., is a professor at Loma Linda University in Loma Linda, California. He earned his Ph.D. in health education from the University of Oregon in 1973. He specializes in consumer health education and biomedical research methodology. For more than thirty years, he has studied the reasons people become victims or proponents of quackery in medicine.

Dr. Jarvis is the editor, author, or co-author of more than 100 publications on topics related to consumer health, including the *American Medical Association's Reader's Guide to "Alternative" Health Methods* and the college textbook *Consumer Health: A Guide to Intelligent Decisions* (6th Ed.).

CHAPTER FOUR

Common Misconceptions About Alternative Medicine

with Edzard Ernst, M.D., Ph.D., FRCP

"Alternative" (also known as "complementary") medicine can be loosely defined as medicine that lies, for the most part, outside the mainstream of scientific biomedicine. Because the term *alternative* encompasses so many therapies, making generalizations about it can be difficult or problematic. What's more, debates about the usefulness of alternative therapies often are emotional and unproductive.

In hopes that a more useful approach can be found, this chapter will point out some of the main arguments used by both sides of the debate. It will also try to clear up some common misconceptions.

ARGUMENTS IN FAVOR OF ALTERNATIVE MEDICINE

THE EFFECTS OF ALTERNATIVE MEDICINE ARE PROVEN. In the veterinary literature, this is certainly not the case. Still, some studies suggest that certain treatments can affect bodily functions; for example, acupuncture may increase horses' levels of endorphins, the naturally occurring opiumlike compounds in the body.

Even though evidence may exist to support a treatment's claim, contradictory evidence also may exist (in the case of acupuncture, evidence might show that it doesn't increase endorphin levels). Furthermore, apparently supportive findings may be meaningless. For example, even if you could determine that acupuncture increases endorphin levels, you couldn't necessarily go the next step and conclude that acupuncture is an effective means of pain management; you couldn't even conclude that it matters where you insert the needles. To be considered useful, a treatment must be shown to work through proper scientific trials, and these trials are virtually nonexistent in equine veterinary medicine.

ALL THAT MATTERS IS THAT THE PATIENT IS HELPED. This commonly heard argument sounds powerful and convincing: Almost any means of treatment is justified, as long as it helps horses. If your horse has an ailment that can't be cured, "alternative" therapies at least offer some comfort and hope. Of course, comfort and hope can be provided by just about anyone, including mainstream practitioners. False hope, on the other hand, can be tragically deceiving.

There are other reasons why the "as long as it helps" argument is flawed. If people believe that they can treat a condition with an unproven treatment, that belief may slow the progress of future research into that condition. Furthermore, if placebo effects cause a horse owner to believe that the animal's condition (which would have improved anyway, regardless of the treatment) improved because of the treatment, what will happen if the horse later develops a truly serious health problem? Will the owner delay getting the horse effective treatment because he or she has put trust in the ineffective treatment?

FREEDOM OF THERAPEUTIC CHOICE MUST NOT BE SACRIFICED. True, but this mandate should apply only to effective therapies. If ineffective treatments continue to persist under "freedom of choice," how are you supposed to know how to choose?

ALTERNATIVE MEDICINE IS NATURAL AND THEREFORE HARMLESS. Many people believe so; some doctors and alternative therapy practitioners apparently think so, too. But there is no such thing as a treatment with absolutely no potential to do harm. A toxic or contaminated herbal remedy, for example, could be directly harmful. Some treatments may have side effects; horses have been injured by chiropractic manipulations and have reacted aggressively to the insertion of acupuncture needles. In addition, the use of alternative therapies may cause harm if it prevents or delays the use of proven, effective treatments or, as with any therapy, if it's employed by an incompetent practitioner.

ALTERNATIVE MEDICINE PROVES ITS WORTH EVERY DAY. Alternative medicine practitioners regularly say words to this effect. Veterinarians and horse owners alike tend to credit the chosen treatment with the subsequent improvement. Of course, to do so is to forget to consider other possible reasons that symptoms improved. Forgetting that experience alone can be misleading may well have created more believers in unproven therapies than any other single factor.

ALTERNATIVE THERAPIES HAVE STOOD THE TEST OF TIME. The history books are filled with accounts of long-standing remedies, such as blood-letting, that for many years were considered effective and eventually were proven worthless or even harmful. Furthermore, the "test of time" argument can be turned around on alternative therapies: If they have been around for such a long time, why has nobody been able to prove their effectiveness?

ALTERNATIVE THERAPIES CANNOT OR SHOULD NOT BE TESTED SCIENTIFICALLY. You may hear the following justifications:

- Current technology can't detect alternative therapies' subtle effects.

- Science isn't studying the correct responses when it comes to alternative therapies.

- Group studies on the effects of alternative therapies in horses are inconclusive because each individual is unique.

- It's unethical to do a placebo-controlled trial when you know a therapy works.

Even if there were truth to each of these statements, these are the same issues that any scientific investigation has to deal with. However, there's no reason that any therapeutic effect should disappear under a properly controlled scientific trial.

ONLY ALTERNATIVE MEDICINE CONCERNS ITSELF WITH THE WHOLE HORSE. This argument makes science-minded veterinarians crazy. It tries to separate alternative medicine from the mainstream on principle. It asserts that conventional medicine is concerned only with the part of the horse that's sick, injured, or lame; but alternative medicine sees the horse in terms of his wider surroundings. The idea that a veterinarian should be concerned with the whole patient is hardly an invention of alternative medicine. On the other hand, saying that everything can potentially affect a horse makes it difficult to tell what's important from what isn't, so such an approach isn't likely to be of much help in determining the appropriate treatment.

ARGUMENTS AGAINST ALTERNATIVE MEDICINE

ALTERNATIVE MEDICINE IS UNSCIENTIFIC; ORTHODOX MEDICINE IS SCIENTIFIC. Modern medicine is defined by the scientific method. In historical terms, though, the application of science to mainstream medicine is relatively new. As a result, even some conventional medical and veterinary treatments fail to meet the requirements of science. However, the scientific foundations of alternative medicine are even shakier than those of orthodox medicine. Some researchers are currently attempting to subject some forms of alternative medicine to scientific scrutiny. For instance, about 2,000 controlled clinical trials of alternative treatment modalities have been conducted with human subjects.

ALTERNATIVE MEDICINE IS KNOWN TO BE INEFFECTIVE. This idea may be the most prevalent prejudice against alternative medicine. It's true that some "alternative" diagnostic techniques, such as attempting to detect disease by examining the iris of the eye or analyzing hair, are absolutely worthless. But to make such a broad generalization is itself unscientific. If a therapy is untested, you can't say whether it's effective. Furthermore, some studies of alternative medicines do suggest that certain therapies may be useful.

THE PHILOSOPHIES OF ALTERNATIVE MEDICINE ARE SO OBVIOUSLY FLAWED THAT SCIENTIFIC TESTING WOULD BE A WASTE OF TIME. Alternative medicine often lacks a sound theoretical basis. But by their very nature philosophies, like religions, cannot be proven right or wrong. Although classifying some of these philosophies as myths is probably correct, the remedies associated with the philosophies are not necessarily useless.

ALTERNATIVE MEDICINE IS NOTHING MORE THAN A PLACEBO. The apparent success of some alternative therapies, despite the lack of supporting evidence, puzzles many practitioners. If you assume that alternative medicines are bogus, you may be tempted to credit their effects to a powerful placebo response, but the mere fact that some such treatments have produced documented side effects suggests that some are more than mere placebos.

ONLY A SMALL MINORITY OF PEOPLE USE ALTERNATIVE MEDICINE FOR THEIR HORSES. This argument is used to downplay the importance of the entire alternative medicine issue, but it's not necessarily true. It's impossible to estimate how many horse owners use alternative therapies, but human medical studies suggest that a significant number of people use them for themselves. Alternative therapies need to be taken seriously, both from a medical standpoint and in economic terms.

ORTHODOX MEDICINE HAS NOTHING TO LEARN FROM ALTERNATIVE MEDICINE. Horse owners consult with alternative therapy practitioners for many reasons, from disappointment in established therapies to an inclination to believe in mysticism. Whatever their reasons, they represent a serious critique of the style of orthodox medicine. Veterinarians may need to learn lessons about having time and caring for their clients, maximizing placebo effects by offering reassurance when warranted, and considering seriously even minor complaints. It may simply come down to a revival of good doctoring.

WHERE DO WE GO FROM HERE?

First, if people truly want to help horses, both orthodox and alternative practitioners must get past their prejudices. Neither blind faith in a therapy nor stubborn disbelief is going to help.

Second, both sides need to be aware of the facts. For starters, proponents and opponents of alternative medicine might think about stopping the habit of selectively quoting only those particular bits of evidence that support their positions. There's always more than one side to an argument.

Third, more and better research is urgently needed. That research should systematically address how well the therapies work, their safety, and their cost-effectiveness.

Fourth, research takes money. Although the funds available for equine research are paltry when compared to those for human medical research, monies do exist.

PUBLICATION BIAS

A problem in trying to review the medical literature on alternative therapies is *publication bias*, a phenomenon that rears its head in all scholarly journals: Studies that show positive results are more likely to be published than those that are inconclusive or show negative results. A 1997 report in the journal *Nature* reviewed more than 200 articles printed in four alternative medicine journals and found that only 1 percent were negative. In a 1998 review, the journal *Controlled Clinical Trials* concluded that 100 percent of Chinese studies of acupuncture showed positive results. These and other similar figures suggest that the literature on alternative therapies may not be entirely objective.

Answering the questions that alternative medicine presents won't be easy, and it won't happen quickly. It would help if both sides of the discussion would get together to speed the process. If you combine enthusiasm for a therapy with a scientific approach and expertise, you have a great recipe for finding the answers.

EDZARD ERNST

Edzard Ernst, M.D., Ph.D., FRCP, has been a professor of physical medicine and rehabilitation at the Universities of Hanover (Germany) and Vienna (Austria). He now chairs the Department of Alternative and Complementary Medicine at England's University of Exeter. His clinical experience includes angiology, complementary medicine, hemorheology, internal medicine, physical medicine, rehabilitation and psychiatry. He serves as an external examiner for the Universities of Bombay, London, Ulster and Manchester Metropolitan and is the editor-in-chief of three medical journals.

CHAPTER FIVE

The Ethics of Providing Therapy

with Bernard E. Rollin, Ph.D.

Why ethics? Isn't this subject out of place in a book on alternative therapies? Not at all. Therapy, like any other aspect of life, is subject to rules that govern right and wrong, good and bad, justice and injustice. In order for society to function without chaos and anarchy, rules must exist that govern and constrain our conduct. Some of these rules are articulated in a social consensus ethic that is usually written in law (such as laws prohibiting murder, rape and discrimination). Other rules, such as a person's choice to worship or to give to charity, are a matter of personal ethics.

A third category, which relates directly to the practice of medicine, is professional ethics, the rules that govern the behavior of physicians, veterinarians and others who perform special and vital functions in society and are granted such special privileges as prescribing medications and performing surgery. Because society as a whole does not understand the complexities of such professions, it tends to avoid passing laws that regulate professionals' behavior; instead, it allows professionals to govern themselves, with the proviso that they do so in a way that meets social expectations.

The issue of what constitutes good and legitimate therapy is a very serious question in veterinary medical ethics. If you enlist the services of a professional to help care for your horse, you have entered into a contract with that person. You expect the professional not to take advantage of you or your horse, to respect you and your animal, to help and to do no harm and to act with a sense of fairness. Meeting all of these expectations requires the professional to practice sound professional ethics.

CAVEAT EMPTOR AND CAVEAT VENDOR

In medieval times, people purchased goods and services by bartering, and everybody knew (or was presumed to know) the worth of these things. As a result, the onus was on the buyer to make sure that he or she was getting a good deal. Thus was born the basic principle of "buyer beware" (*caveat emptor*).

As the scope of commerce grew, it became impossible for consumers to know everything about the goods for which they were trading. The laws and the social ethic began to recognize that consumers can't bargain knowledgeably for something of which they cannot be expected to know the value. In the fifteenth century, the principle of commerce shifted from *caveat emptor* to *caveat vendor* (seller beware). "Seller beware" implies that the seller is obligated to protect the interests of the buyer. This principle has been upheld legally, meaning that if a seller of goods or services takes advantage of you, that person may be legally liable for the consequences.

Obviously, if you knew how to fix your horse's problem, you'd do so yourself. But you can't know everything, and so you have to trust that the professional you hire to treat the problem behaves ethically. If you investigate the person's professional ethics before you engage her services, you'll help ensure your horse's welfare. Signs of ethical professional behavior are described in the following sections.

RESPECT FOR YOUR WISHES

There are usually at least two people involved in a decision to start therapy—you and the therapy provider—and at least one horse. The person that is giving you a hand has the obligation to respect your wishes, assuming that your wishes have been made known after careful consideration (it's not just a matter of the care provider agreeing with your wishes like some sort of a doll with a bobbing head). You own the horse; you hold the cards. Even so, although the care provider has a moral obligation to respect your wishes, he or she also has an equal obligation to look after your horse.

Respecting your wishes makes the person who is helping you obliged to follow certain ethical paths. After all, you may only wish for the best care but you may not know what that "best" care might be. So, the care provider has an obligation to listen to your concerns and to make sure that you are fully informed about the risks, benefits and validity of a therapy before starting to treat your horse. Your consent to have a therapy must be given with full and reliable information so that you can make an informed decision. On the other hand, you may not *want* a lot of information. In those cases, you need to tell the care provider that you want to leave the decision in his or her hands.

It's also mandatory that whoever you choose not deceive you (intentionally or otherwise). The lack of deceit is implied by the principle of respecting your wishes. You have an absolute right to get the truth about a certain condition or therapy and the person who fails to give it to you is nothing less than a fraud or incompetent. If you're desperate to find something to help your horse, it is clearly unethical for someone to promote an unproven therapy just so they can help relieve you of some of your spare cash. While this concept may seem obvious, the potential for abuse in this area is tremendous, especially when you are dealing with untrained and/or unlicensed practitioners of a therapy.

THE INTERESTS OF THE VETERINARIAN

The person that you've asked to take care of your horse has an interest in this transaction, as well. Veterinary medicine is based on veterinary science. Through this system of objectively validating therapies, veterinarians have gained the respect and trust of horse owners. Veterinary science should ensure that your horse's condition has been diagnosed, that the treatment that is being provided your horse is specific for your horse's condition and that the effects of the treatment are better than just waiting around and seeing what happens. Since "alternative" therapies are generally unproven therapies, your veterinarian may feel ethically bound not to provide them. Thus, many veterinarians may be against the application of unproven therapies even if you want to give them a try. So if the veterinarian feels that the treatment that you want to try is against the best interests of the horse or isn't proven, he or she may feel morally *obliged* to refuse your request. Of course, if there is evidence that the treatment that you want to do is harmful, for a veterinarian to agree to apply it would also be unethical. As a client, you in turn, are ethically bound to respect his or her wishes in those circumstances.

However, some remedies, while unproven, may not be harmful at all. You may just feel like you know what's best for your horse or that you want to try some sort of an "alternative" therapy. If there's no demonstrable harm, and if you want to give it a try, there may not be much good reason for the veterinarian to turn you down (and it might just provoke a fight). After all, it's your money and if you want to spend it on an unproven therapy, you do have that right. Still, before you make any such decision, you should consult with your veterinarian (and/or other veterinarians) to try to find out about the potential risks and benefits of the treatment in question.

The fact that a particular therapy is or is not proven may not even be important to you. It may not matter to you if you're seeing a real effect from the treatment or if you just feel better because you think that you are doing something to "help." But the treatment's scientific basis (or lack thereof) may make a *big* difference to the person who is providing the therapy, as well as to the horse (of course). If a veterinarian administers (and charges for) a treatment that has no demonstrable effect, he or she may feel that you're just being deceived. That's an ethical no-no all the way around.

If you demand that your veterinarian provide a therapy for your horse in which he or she has no confidence, you're putting your veterinarian in a very difficult position. You may be asking him or her to do something that their science and ethics say should not be done. That's not something that you can ethically ask of them. However, if your veterinarian doesn't do what you want, you may go somewhere else (and veterinarians know this). If you persist in your demands, you will undoubtedly find someone who *will* do what you want, but be aware that doing so may not be in the best interests of you *or* the horse!

FAIRNESS

Fairness is the moral obligation to do the right thing personally, professionally and for society in an impartial, non–self-serving way. On a personal level, you and your veterinary care provider should avoid any practice for which there is no moral imperative or justification. For example, a provider's selling you a product just because doing so is profitable is taking advantage of your good faith. It's also not fair for a provider to sell you a more-expensive product or service if a less-expensive product or service will do just as well.

Similarly, it's not fair for your veterinary care provider to overexamine or underexamine your horse; the diagnostic services provided should be appropriate to your complaint. If your horse has a hoof abscess, for example, suggesting numerous radiographs may be unethical. Your veterinary care provider should be competent enough to provide a reasonable diagnosis. He or she also should be aware of the limitations of his or her experience, even if that means referring you to another practitioner.

Last, both you and your veterinary care provider must obey local, state and national laws. If the law states that veterinarians must notify the authorities of horses diagnosed with public-health threats such as equine infectious anemia, rabies and vesicular stomatitis, your veterinarian must do so even if you protest. Similarly, if the law states that only licensed veterinarians are allowed to practice veterinary medicine, you must respect that law. You may believe that it is wrong for a chiropractor to be prevented from treating horses unless supervised by a veterinarian; you may even feel morally entitled to break the law. But if you do so, both you and the chiropractor have to be ready to face the consequences. In addition, a veterinarian who observes the chiropractor breaking the law may feel ethically bound to report the offense to the proper authorities.

DOING NO HARM AND DOING SOME GOOD

The first basic rule of medicine is: Above all, do no harm. No procedure, device or therapy should expose your horse to more risk than the condition itself poses. Of course, ethical treatment means more than simply not hurting the horse: It means helping the horse, which comes back to the issue of choosing a treatment that's been proven effective.

In any medical or veterinary practice, the threat of malpractice or incompetence exists. It seems logical that untrained or unlicensed practitioners are more likely than trained, certified practitioners to do harm. If your care provider is not licensed and regulated, you have no recourse if something should go wrong. You may assume that an unlicensed provider has sufficient ethical standards, but this is not always the case. If you engage the services of such an individual, it's back to "let the buyer beware."

SAFE AND EFFECTIVE PRACTICES

Further ethical considerations require that proof of a therapy's effectiveness be established if the safety and efficacy questions have not been documented. Although no effective therapy exists without some potential of harm, however slight, you need to know its risks and benefits in order to make an informed decision about using it. It's nearly impossible to conduct this sort of risk/benefit analysis for alternative therapies because neither the potential risks nor the potential benefits have been fully evaluated in an objective, scientific fashion.

Morality and common courtesy dictate that you be fully informed as to whether a therapy is experimental or unproven before your horse receives it. If such information is not disclosed in advance, you have reason to suspect the practitioner's ethics.

It would also seem reasonable to expect that if someone intends to use an unproven therapy, that person is ethically obligated to engage in or encourage the necessary clinical research to establish or disprove its effectiveness. It's not up to the people who don't use a therapy to show that it doesn't work; it's up to the providers of that therapy to show that it does.

DISCLOSURE OF PROVEN ALTERNATIVES

It is unethical to use an unproven therapy if an established, effective treatment for the condition already exists or if you risk causing your horse additional suffering if the unproven therapy fails. For instance, you may consider antibiotics to be unnatural or overprescribed (and you may well be right). But if your horse is sick and antibiotics are the most effective treatment, using an unproven alternative therapy instead may cause harm—clearly an unacceptable and unethical decision.

THE COSTS OF UNPROVEN TREATMENT

For a variety of reasons, most veterinary experts don't like to recommend unproven therapies. However, promoters of such therapies often criticize their reserve as overly cautious or conservative. They suggest that if a treatment is harmless, there's no reason to stop people from giving it a try. If it does work, even better! In other words, they suggest that the potential benefits outweigh the potential risks.

There are some big problems with this argument, which fails to take into account some important questions: How likely is it that the treatment will work? Can the treatment do any harm? Simple probability statistics dictate that new or unproven therapies are more likely to be ineffective than effective. So the odds are excellent that the people who pay for those therapies are wasting their time and money. The pro-unproven-therapy argument also doesn't account for the possibility of direct harm (from adverse reactions or physical injury) or indirect harm (if an unproven therapy is chosen instead of a proven one). It also fails to acknowledge the very real emotional harm done to the horse owner who realizes he or she has been sold false hope.

COST-AWARENESS

As you know, it costs money to take proper care of your horse. If it becomes ill or injured, you may have little choice but to spend extra money on veterinary care. Most horse owners will swallow hard and spend whatever's necessary to ensure their animal's well-being, but there are no bonus points for paying for products and services that aren't clearly required. Unless you are independently wealthy, you may find yourself unable to afford that new saddle or that clinic or horse show if you spend all your horse money on unproven therapies. In addition, any practitioner who takes advantage of your well-meaning desire to help your horse by selling you unnecessary procedures or treatments is acting unethically.

REGARD FOR THE INTERESTS OF SOCIETY

Everyone who loves horses wants them to be sound and healthy and for their ailments to be treated as safely, effectively and economically as possible. If you do decide to have an alternative therapy practitioner treat your horse, keep your regular veterinarian informed as to what's being done. That way, if there is genuine improvement, it can be documented and potentially investigated. Furthermore, your veterinarian can make sure a treatment isn't inadvertently administered that could produce harmful side effects when combined with the alternative treatment. He or she may also have some idea of where to look in the event that the alternative treatment goes awry. If you can get the various practitioners to work together, you're more likely to come away with some benefit for your horse.

Above all, act in your horse's best interests. No one is saying that all alternative therapies lack value or that all established therapies are perfect and 100 percent effective. But if no objective evidence exists to support a therapy's safety and efficacy, using it can't be justified rationally. As a horse owner who wants the best for your animal, you are morally obligated to choose a therapy that is supported by evidence over one that has not been tested and may be neither safe nor effective.

BERNARD ROLLIN

Bernard Rollin, Ph.D., is a professor of philosophy, physiology and biophysics and is the director of bioethical planning at Colorado State University. He was a Fulbright Fellow at the University of Edinburgh from 1964 to 1965 and received his Ph.D. from Columbia University in 1972. He taught the world's first course in veterinary medical ethics and has been a pioneer in reforming animal use in surgery teaching and laboratory exercises in veterinary colleges. He is a principal architect of 1985 U.S. federal legislation dealing with the welfare of experimental animals, has testified before

Congress on animal experimentation and has consulted with the governments of five foreign countries on many aspects of animal research. He is the author of more than 175 papers and ten books, including *Animal Rights and Human Morality,* which won an Outstanding Book of the Year Award from the American Association of University Libraries.

CHAPTER SIX

Energy Medicine

with Victor J. Stenger, Ph.D.

Much alternative medicine is grounded in *vitalism*, the notion that living organisms possess some unique quality, an *élan vital*, that gives them that special quality called life. Belief in the existence of a life force is ancient and remains widespread to this day. Called *prana* by the Hindus, *qi* or *chi* by the Chinese and *ki* by the Japanese (to mention but a few), this substance is often associated with the soul, the spirit and the mind.

In ancient times, the vital force was widely identified with breathing, which the Hebrews called *ruach*, the Greeks *psyche* or *pneuma* ("the breath of the gods") and the Romans *spiritus*. Breath was eventually acknowledged to be a material substance, yet words such as *psychic* and *spirit* came to refer to the assumed nonmaterial and perhaps even supernatural medium that bestows life and consciousness on organisms. The idea that matter alone can do the job has never proved popular.

THE PERMUTATIONS OF ENERGY MEDICINE

From its ancient roots, the concept of a special life force has found many expressions. Over time, those concepts have been expanded and developed in a virtually endless number of ways. Mystical energy forms are everywhere in the annals of alternative medicine.

CHINESE MEDICINE

The concept of *qi* remains in traditional Chinese medicine, which is experiencing an upsurge of interest in the West as a result of people's interest in acupuncture. *Qi* is a mysterious life force that is said to flow rhythmically through so-called meridians in the body. Acupuncture and acupressure are said to stimulate the flow of *qi* at special acupoints along these meridians. What's more, the *qi* force is not limited to the body but is believed to flow through one's environment. For example, many believers in Chinese medicine consult with masters of *feng shui* (the practice of living harmoniously with the energy of the surrounding environment) before they build their houses. The masters help them orient the building, its interior design, and the furniture in a manner that aligns with the *qi* force.

NEWTONIAN ALCHEMY

As modern science developed in the West and researchers began to understand the nature of matter, a few scientists tried to find evidence of the nature of the living force. After Sir Isaac Newton published his laws of mechanics, optics, and gravity in the 1700s, he spent many years conducting alchemic experiments in hopes of finding the source of life. Newtonian physics couldn't explain the complexity necessary in any purely material theory of life or mind (doing so requires quantum physics—see "A Short Primer on Quantum Mechanics" later in this chapter). Even Newtonian gravity theory had an occult quality about it, because gravity is a mysterious, invisible action that appears to be transmitted across space. However, Newton and others who followed never managed to find hard evidence for a special substance of spirit or life.

Mesmer and Magnetism

In the eighteenth century, the Austrian physician Franz Anton Mesmer advanced the theory that magnetism is the universal life force. He treated a wide variety of ills with magnets in the belief that a force called *animal magnetism* resides in the human body and can be directed into other bodies—a theory that's alive and well today. Mesmer's patients would exhibit violent reactions when he "directed his energy" toward them by pointing his finger, until the flow of "nervous current" would rebalance the patients' energies. Today, *mesmerism* is associated with hypnosis rather than with animal magnetism or other notions of a life force, but Mesmer's ideas have survived in various holistic theories that contradict established science.

Parapsychology

In the late nineteenth century, prominent scientists such as William Crookes and Oliver Lodge sought to prove the existence of what they called the "psychic force," which they believed was responsible for the mysterious powers of the mind being exhibited by mediums and spiritualist hucksters. They thought the psychic force might be related to the electromagnetic "aether waves" that had just been discovered and were being put to amazing use.

After all, if wireless telegraphy was possible, why not wireless telepathy? Although this question seemed reasonable at the time, wireless telepathy failed to advance in the full century of poorly conducted parapsychology experiments that followed.

MIND OVER MATTER?

An Associated Press story from 1989 illustrates the tragic consequences of overestimating one's ability to control energy:

> E. Frenkel, one of the Soviet Union's growing number of psychic healers and mentalists, claimed he used his powers to stop bicycles, automobiles and streetcars. He thought he was ready for stopping something bigger, so he stepped in front of a freight train. It didn't work.
>
> The engineer of the train that ran Frenkel over said the psychic stepped onto the tracks with his arms raised, his head lowered and his body tensed.
>
> The daily Sovietskaya Rossiya yesterday said investigators looking into Frenkel's decision to jump in front of a train near the southern city of Astrakhan found the answer in the briefcase he left by the side of the track. "First I stopped a bicycle, cars, and a streetcar," Frenkel wrote in notes that the investigators found. "Now I'm going to stop a train."[1]

Frenkel apparently thought he had found the secret of psychic-biological power and that his attempt to halt a train would be the ultimate test of his powers, according to his notes. "Only in extraordinary conditions of a direct threat to my organism will all my reserves be called into action," he wrote.

THE CONTINUING APPEAL
OF LIFE-FORCE THEORIES

Scientific medicine follows established fields such as biology, chemistry and physics in its approach to studying, diagnosing and treating the material body. The array of modern diagnostic gadgets—ultrasound, radiographs, bone scans and the like—and of drugs and medicines reinforces the image of the veterinarian as a sort of equine mechanic, who just fixes broken parts. It's no surprise that practitioners who purport to go beyond the mechanics and treat the whole horse find many eager listeners. A ready market exists for therapists who claim they can succeed in cases where medical science fails.

BIOENERGETIC FIELDS

These days, the vital force is often referred to as the *bioenergetic field*. In biochemistry, the term *bioenergetic* refers to readily measurable exchanges of energy. These exchanges, which occur within organisms and between them and their environment, take place as a result of normal, measurable physical and chemical processes.

Touch therapists, acupuncturists, chiropractors and other alternative practitioners claim that they can affect cures for many ills by manipulating this field, thereby bringing the body's live energies into balance. The new vitalists imagine the bioenergetic field as a holistic life force that goes beyond physics and chemistry. Used in this sense, holistic refers to more than the whole-patient approach.

Psychological, emotional and social factors, in addition to a person's physical health, help determine a person's sense of well-being. So-called holistic practitioners also cite these factors, but they imply that their treatments themselves somehow address all of them. In truth, your horse's body is a system, and it's impossible to treat one part without affecting others, no matter what therapy you choose. But holistic practitioners believe that your horse's bioenergetic field is a cosmic force that pervades the universe and acts instantaneously, faster than the speed of light, over all of space.

In a chapter titled "Energy Medicine" in a recently published book, *Complementary and Alternative Veterinary Medicine*, the author writes: "The principles of energy medicine originate in quantum physics. Bioenergetic medicine is the study of human and animal bodies as dynamic electromagnetic fields existing in an electromagnetic environment."

The above statement is problematic, for a number of reasons. The author fails to specify or even guess at the exact nature of the bioenergetic field. "Bioenergetic medicine" seems to be equated to the classical electromagnetic field; forget the fact that dynamic electromagnetic fields are easy to measure. Such statements are nonsensical. Elegant, perhaps, but nonsense nonetheless.

AURAS AND DISCHARGES

Some energy medicine advocates describe the bioenergetic field as a special form of electromagnetism, advancing as evidence the measurable electromagnetic waves emitted by humans. They believe in the existence of a universal energy field of which we are all part—thus the notion of "spiritual healing." Some people call these individual life forces or energy fields *auras*. Some self-proclaimed psychics claim to be able to see others' auras, although such claims have frequently been disproven.

Living things do have auras, but those auras aren't mysterious. Living bodies emit what's known as *black body electromagnetic radiation.* This invisible light is caused by heat-activated movement of the body's charged particles and can be photographed with infrared-sensitive film. Fanciful shapes visible in photographed auras can be completely attributed to optical and photographic effects.

Other creative explanations of auras and discharges suppose that bacteria, viruses and other invaders possess electromagnetic fields that can weaken our cells. Changes in our energy fields, the theory goes, lead to disease; bioenergetic therapies can restore the balance of our life energies. Such effects have never been demonstrated.

SCIENCE'S VIEW

The effects of electromagnetic fields in living things should be easy to detect, given the great precision with which researchers can measure electromagnetic phenomena. Physics, a science that can measure the magnetic dipole moment of the electron (a measure of the strength of the electron's magnetic field) to one part in ten *billion,* surely should be able to detect any electromagnetic effects in the body powerful enough to move atoms around or do whatever happens in causing or curing disease.

The brain and certain other organs do emit electromagnetic waves at a range of frequencies, and bioenergists point to these waves as evidence for the basis of their methods. But these waves show no characteristics to differentiate them from the electromagnetic waves produced by moving charges in any electronic system; they can be simulated with a computer. Studies have not shown even a hint of the existence of any special form of energy unique to living systems.

KIRLIAN PHOTOGRAPHY

A special kind of photography often is cited as evidence for the existence of life fields. In 1937, Semyon Davidovich Kirlian, an Armenian electrician, discovered that photographs of living things placed in a high-pulse electromagnetic field reveal a remarkable aura. In the typical Kirlian experiment, a freshly cut leaf is placed on a piece of film that is electrically isolated from a flat aluminum electrode. High-pulse electrical voltage is then applied between another electrode placed in contact with the leaf and the aluminum electrode. When the film is developed, the photographs reveal dynamic, changing patterns, including multicolored sparks, twinkles and flares. As the leaf dies, the patterns gradually disappear.

Despite the method's apparently convincing evidence, it's been amply demonstrated that the Kirlian aura is a corona discharge of electricity, which is greater when an object has a high moisture content (the just-picked leaf) than after it dries. You can wet a piece of dead wood and achieve the same effect.

ALTERNATIVE ENERGY SOURCES

It's not irrational to propose that there are as-yet-undiscovered kinds of energy. If it were, it would have been irrational to propose the existence of electric fields in the 1800s or of the

strong nuclear force in the 1900s. The problem lies in finding evidence of the existence of the new energy.

QUANTUM HEALING

Practically every book or article about alternative therapies mentions the term *quantum*. Quantum physics attempts to predict the
behavior of particles that are smaller than atoms. These particles
sometimes act in ways that appear inconsistent with the principles
of Newtonian physics. Because of this apparently random behavior, some people have suggested that nothing is certain. The term
quantum seems to be used to make all of the inconsistencies, inco-
herencies and incompatibilities in a weird theory disappear in a
puff of smoke. Because quantum physics is strange, anything that
is strange must be quantum physics.

Nothing could be further from the truth. The principles of
quantum mechanics apply only at very small distances, such as
inside atoms, or in very special macroscopic circumstances, such as
occur in superconductivity. Furthermore, even those quantum phenomena that seem to violate established physical principles still
can be explained in material, scientific terms. Nothing that is
known about quantum mechanics requires the introduction of
mystical elements as an explanation.

Quantum theory has virtually no significance at the biological
or even microbiological level. Nevertheless, mind-over-matter
solutions to health problems (known as *quantum healing*) are often

justified through inaccurate references to quantum mechanics. This concept is extended to imply that human consciousness controls reality, and so people can think themselves healthy or even immortal. Some writers of alternative medical literature assert that evidence exists for some entity beyond conventional matter and that modern physical theory, particularly quantum mechanics, supports this evidence.

Much as some people might wish otherwise, no unique life force has been conclusively demonstrated to exist. Claims of evidence of the existence of a life force do not meet any reasonable application of scientific criteria; not even the most powerful electron microscopes, the most sensitive electromagnetic detectors nor particle accelerators reveal any evidence of its existence. The bioenergetic field plays no role in the theory or practice of biology or science-based medicine. Practitioners whose methods call for the existence of such a field have an enormous burden of proof, and it is time that society laid it on their thin shoulders.

A SHORT PRIMER ON QUANTUM MECHANICS

By the end of the nineteenth century, only a few rare phenomena appeared inconsistent with the theoretical structure of physics that had developed from the time of Sir Isaac Newton. A new theory was needed to explain these phenomena, and that theory became known as quantum mechanics.

In 1900, Max Planck introduced the concept that light occurs in discrete bundles of energy, or *quanta*, in an effort to explain the spectrum of radiation from bodies. In 1905, Albert Einstein proposed that these quanta were particles (now called photons), thereby explaining why light produces an electric current, a phenomenon known as the photoelectric effect.

In 1913, Niels Bohr used quantum theory to calculate the energy levels of the hydrogen atom, arguing that the electron circles the nucleus in only certain, discrete orbits. In 1923, Louis de Broglie proposed that electrons have wave-like properties, a theory that experiments soon confirmed. De Broglie's discovery led to the wave-particle duality, in which objects are somehow regarded as being both waves and particles; the wave-particle duality itself then led to the development of formal mathematical theories of quantum mechanics by Werner Heisenberg and Erwin Schrödinger.

Quantum mechanics introduced a randomness into the universe that is still being argued. It also forced scientists to rethink some of their conceptions of the nature of reality. Two notions of quantum are frequently misunderstood and misused, however. First, quantum mechanics did not show that Newtonian mechanics is wrong. Most physical phenomena, including most of what goes on inside living bodies, can be understood with Newtonian mechanics. Second, those quantum phenomena that seem to violate normal common sense can still be understood in purely material, physical terms. Although mystical elements have been proposed, nothing that is known about quantum requires us to introduce such elements. The bottom line remains: quantum mechanics agrees with all observations.

VICTOR J. STENGER

Victor J. Stenger is a professor of physics and astronomy at the University of Hawaii. He received his Ph.D. from the University of California at Los Angeles in 1963 and since then has had an active research career in elementary particle physics and astrophysics. He has been a visiting professor at the University of Heidelberg, Oxford University, Rutherford-Appleton Laboratory, and the Italian National Institute for Nuclear Research. He was one of the pioneers in the development of high-energy gamma-ray and neutrino astronomy. He is currently a collaborator on Super-Kamiokande, an experiment in a mine in Japan that has recently reported the observation of neutrino mass.

Dr. Stenger has written about subjects ranging from alternative medicine to psychic phenomena and quantum mysticism. He is the author of three critically acclaimed books, *Not by Design: The Origin of the Universe*; *Physics and Psychics: The Search for a World Beyond the Senses*; and *The Unconscious Quantum: Metaphysics in Modern Physics and Cosmology*.

NOTE

1. Associated Press. Article in *The Morning Call*, October 2, 1989, page A7.

CHAPTER SEVEN

Acupuncture

with Stephen Basser, M.B., B.S.;
Jack Raso, M.S., R.D.; and Wallace Sampson, M.D., FACOP

The practice of acupuncture is fairly new to Western veterinary medicine; it was introduced in the United States in the early 1970s. Of all of the modes of alternative medicine available to horse owners, it is perhaps the most mysterious, elusive and difficult to sum up.

Although acupuncture is generally thought of as an ancient component of Chinese medicine, it has dozens of forms and variations that are neither ancient nor Chinese. Historically, the practice of acupuncture was based on the belief that the body is subject to disease when its vital force (known as *qi* or *chi*) becomes "unbalanced". The classical technique involves placing fine needles at specific points in the body in an effort to restore that "balance." The selection of points relates loosely to the patient's symptoms and closely to the philosophy of the practitioner.

The many variations in the practice of acupuncture include the injection of saline or other solutions (such as vitamin B_{12} or corticosteroids) at the site of treatment, laser acupuncture and electrical acupuncture. All share the basic premise that various superficial points are therapeutically important. At present, they are all forms of scientifically unproven therapies.

ACUPUNCTURE'S ROLE IN CHINESE HISTORY

Proponents of acupuncture tend to assert that the practice is part of a reliable, traditional medical system that has endured without change for 5,000 years or more. This is not true. What is often termed traditional Chinese medicine includes often-contradictory mystical speculations about how the body works. At times, there appear to be as many forms of acupuncture as there are acupuncturists.

The earliest known comprehensive Chinese medical texts, discovered at the Ma-wang-tui graves in 1973 and dating from 168 B.C., make no mention of acupuncture. Acupuncture as human medicine was first described in 90 B.C. in the Shih-ji text, and the earliest veterinary references to the use of acupuncture in horses appear many hundreds of years later.

In the seventeenth century, a French Jesuit, P. P. Harvieu, who had served as a missionary to China, published the first known work on acupuncture in a Western language. A few years later, a Dutch physician, Willem Ten Rhijnem, wrote the first medical essay on acupuncture, based on his observations of its use by the Japanese. Over the years, Western curiosity with acupuncture has waxed and waned; the late twentieth century appears to be the latest period of interest.

In China, however, the philosophy and development of acupuncture largely ceased in the seventeenth century. At least one eighteenth-century text, the *I-hsöeh Yüan Liu Lun* (1757), lamented the loss of traditional acupuncture points and related conduits (also known as *meridians*). In the nineteenth century, the Chinese government banned acupuncture in favor of scientific techniques in an attempt to modernize medicine. Similarly, Japan introduced science-based medicine in the eighteenth century; within 100 years, science-based medicine largely replaced traditional Chinese techniques in Japan.

By the early twentieth century, traditional Chinese medicine was regarded as a historical oddity and was employed mainly in rural areas. By 1912, acupuncture was no longer a subject for examination in China's Imperial Medical Academy. The early Chinese Communist Party expressed considerable antipathy toward the traditional medical approach and claimed that it conflicted with the Party's dedication to science as the way of progress.

The Mao Zedong era saw a resurgence of the techniques of traditional Chinese medicine. When the People's Republic of China was formed in 1949, China's medical services were inadequate, particularly in rural areas. The government was responsible for health care, but it was unable to make conventional medicine available in all areas. It solved the problem by encouraging the use of traditional healing practices, such as acupuncture. By 1968, the Chinese Ministry of Public Health became largely inconsequential and acupuncture, Chinese herbal medicine and other traditional methods became powerful political tools and were used to judge support for the cultural revolution.

Since Mao's time, the practice of medicine in China has become more scientific. Although certain elements of traditional Chinese medicine have been retained, the call for objective scientific evaluation of the claims of traditional treatments is growing. Still, at present, none of the approximately 46 major medical journals published by the Chinese Medical Association is devoted to acupuncture or any of its variations.

Curiously although acupuncture's popularity appears to be setting in the East, it is rising in the West. Reports of acupuncture's supposedly near-miraculous effectiveness have been published in Western medical journals, and interest in this alternative form of treatment has grown rapidly. Only recently, however, has acupuncture come under scientific scrutiny.

ACUPUNCTURE AND CHINESE PHILOSOPHY

The theories behind acupuncture are intertwined with several metaphysical aspects of Chinese tradition. Before you can examine acupuncture as a treatment, you must understand the basis of its philosophy.

QI (CHI)

Traditional Chinese acupuncture and its variations are based on a concept known as *vitalism* (discussed in Chapter 6), a philosophy that asserts the existence of an invisible, intangible and unique life force. In Chinese medicine, this force is called *qi* (also spelled *chi* and pronounced *chee*). The word *qi* derives from the term *hsieh-chi* (evil influences), which itself hearkens back to an ancient Chinese belief that the agents of illness, including the wind, are demons (*hsieh-kuei*). The wind was thought to reside in caves and tunnels; acupuncture literature uses the Chinese word for caves (*hsueh*) to denote holes in the skin through which *qi* flows into and out of the body. Early acupuncturists believed that they could increase or decrease the flow of *qi* by inserting needles into the *hsueh* and thus promote good health.

YIN, YANG, AND THE FIVE ELEMENTS

Most people are familiar with the Chinese expressions *yin* and *yang*, which refer to the traditional belief in cosmic polarity. Historically, illness was often considered to result from lack of balance between these two opposing forces.

Ancient Chinese medicine also contains the doctrine of the Five Phases or Elements (*wu-hsing*), which involves the categorization of natural phenomena, particularly water, fire, metal, wood and soil, into five lines of correspondence. (A sixth component, grain, is also described.) In traditional Chinese medicine, each element is associated with a particular organ system.

Different schools of Chinese medicine applied these concepts in different and even mutually contradictory ways. For example, an organ associated with one element in one system might be associated with another element in a different system. However, the systems were never standardized, and no objective system for obtaining and recording data existed in ancient China. The Five Phases and the yin-yang theory were and are merely subjective perceptions.

VESSELS

The Ma-wang-tui texts describe eleven *mo* or vessels in the body, which were believed to contain blood and *qi*. The texts do not provide any information on how the blood and *qi* move through the vessels or even if the vessels were considered part of an interconnected system.

By the end of the first century B.C., the number of vessels had increased. The most important text of this time, the *Huang-ti nei-ching*, mentions a network of twelve vessels. *Qi* was now thought to flow separately from the blood, through conduits (*jing*) or conduit vessels (*jing-mo*). Many modern writers refer to these vessels as *meridians*, a term that was introduced in the 1940s.

In 1992, a black-lacquered wooden figure with systematic orange-red linear markings was unearthed in a tomb in the Chinese province of Sichuan. The lines on the figure, which dates to the second or first century B.C., represent bodily conduits, but the conduits are consistent with neither those described in ancient Chinese texts nor with current acupuncture philosophy. As far back as the eighteenth century, a Chinese medical philosopher lamented the loss of knowledge of the original conduits. Wherever or whatever the meridians may be in humans, their current alleged locations are clearly not where they started and their numbers vary depending on who you read.

Curiously, reports of meridians in horses don't show up until the 1970s; in fact, there are no descriptions of animal meridians in ancient Chinese texts. Representations of alleged meridian locations in equine acupuncture diagrams are mere extrapolations based on human charts (that's why horses are said to have a gall bladder meridian, even though they have no gall bladder). Of course, what may be therapeutically useful in humans may not necessarily be so for animals. Moreover, there is no consensus—even among practitioners of equine acupuncture—that horses even have meridians.

ACUPOINTS

The word *acupoint* refers to any number of points on or near the surface of a living body that allegedly are susceptible to healthful activation and communicate with internal organs. According to the first known descriptions of the *hsueh* (acupoints) along the vessels, they number 365, which corresponds to the number of days in a year, not to any anatomic study. Other texts cite a different number of acupoints. In human medicine, well over 2,000 acupuncture points have been posited. (The British acupuncturist Felix Mann observed wryly that if the modern texts are to be believed, there is "no skin left which is not an acupuncture point.") In horses, modern accupuncture point locations differ from ancient ones and even the ancient point locations do not agree with each other.

Even the way acupuncture points are treated has changed. Historical texts describe as many as nine types of needles and needling, but the importance of needle type appears to have been lost in modern variants of acupuncture.

INTERNAL CONTRADICTIONS

In human medicine, ancient acupuncturists focused on the vessels, not the acupoints; modern practitioners consider the acupoints to be more important. Western acupuncturists no longer associate meridians with the vascular system, regarding them instead mainly as functional pathways that connect acupoints, however that distinction has not always been clear.

Some acupuncturists insert needles according to the traditional belief that the vessels do not interconnect. However, many of these same practitioners also rely on a technique known as *pulse diagnosis*, which supposedly is used to identify health problems through assessing differences among characters of the pulse. The problem is that taking the pulse for this purpose makes sense only if the flow through the vessels is continuous. If the vessels are not connected, it follows that the pulse of each vessel would have to be taken separately (and this is what was originally described in historical texts).

UNCOMFORTABLE ACUPUNCTURE FACTS

When traditional Chinese acupuncture originated, there was no understanding of physiology, biochemistry or bodily healing mechanisms. Internal surgical procedures had long been taboo in China, and acupuncture points and conduits were developed with no knowledge of anatomy. If a sick person or animal appeared less sick after acupuncture treatment, it was assumed that the treatment had caused the improvement. There was no formal study of diseases and their natural history, and no attempt was made to determine whether the person would have improved without treatment. Many acupuncture treatments have been passed on untested to this day.

The original mystical basis of acupuncture has no connection with the existing base of scientific knowledge:

1. The concept of qi has no basis in physiology and has never been demonstrated. It is not possible to prove that acupuncture works by affecting qi because qi cannot be defined in nonmystical terms.

2. The vessels or meridians along which the needling points are supposedly located have not been shown to exist and do not relate to human or veterinary anatomy. A single French study using a radioactive tracer injected at an acupuncture point concluded that acupuncture channels in humans did indeed exist; a follow-up study showed that the tracer was being drained away along the normal course of blood vessels.

3. Specific acupuncture points have not been shown to exist. Furthermore, devices marketed as means of locating acupoints have proven unreliable.

In view of such facts and contradictions, some modern acupuncture practitioners have abandoned the ancient theories, including those of vessels/meridians and even of the specific acupuncture points. Some Japanese variations of traditional Chinese acupuncture, for example, have never relied on such concepts.

How Might Acupuncture Work?

Acupuncture proponents may assert that clinical experience proves that acupuncture works because their patients improve. They may also point to modern research that demonstrates a relationship between elevated levels of opioid peptides (such as endorphins) or other chemicals and an analgesic effect.

In fact, a number of studies show elevation of various nervous system chemicals following needling. However, any number of stimuli can cause elevated neurochemical levels. For example, your horse's endorphin levels will rise if you put it in a horse trailer or apply a twitch to its nose; in fact, almost any painful stimulus will increase endorphins. What's more, endorphin levels remain elevated only for a couple of hours—a fact that casts doubt on acupuncture proponents' claims that the treatment produces prolonged effects. Finally, a variety of stimuli, including noninvasive methods such as transelectrical nerve stimulation (TENS), have been shown to produce neurochemical changes. There is no evidence that traditional Chinese acupuncture produces a unique or characteristic change in the bodies of either horses or people.

Lack of evidence notwithstanding, some horse owners, riders, and practitioners swear by acupuncture's benefits for both their horses and themselves. Why?

For one, it's entirely possible that acupuncture treatments produce a powerful nonspecific placebo effect. Data from well-designed scientific investigations suggest that acupuncture's nonspecific effects are impressive. Pain, performance, and well-being are largely subjective states. So even if your horse's condition doesn't change following his acupuncture treatment, you might feel better if you believe you've done something to help him. Even simple *counter-irritation*, which is an irritating stimulus that distracts the subject from another irritation, caused by the needle insertion, may be at work.

Scientific evaluations of acupuncture's worth for horses must include an attempt to see whether it relieves pain or other symptoms better than a placebo. Currently, no evidence supports the view that acupuncture has a separate and distinct action or effect that can't be accounted for by any of the previous explanations.

ACUPUNCTURE RESEARCH

Acupuncture has been the subject of a good deal of scientific research, although most of that research has been done on humans. In addition, a number of reviews and *meta-analyses* (studies whose conclusions are drawn from statistic combinations of data from many studies) of acupuncture were published in the 1990s. The data that has emerged is confusing and frequently disappointing to those who believe in acupuncture's effectiveness.

In the 1970s, when acupuncture began gaining popularity in the West, many reports suggested that it was an effective modality. Unfortunately, these good results have not been obtained consistently under rigorous scientific conditions. Although some individual trials suggest that acupuncture has some therapeutic utility, systematic reviews and meta-analyses on the effectiveness of acupuncture in treating pain, addiction and osteoarthritis and in aiding in smoking cessation and weight loss all have concluded that acupuncture is no more effective than placebo treatments.

In any case, if acupuncture produces any sort of therapeutic effect, where the needles are placed may be unimportant. In trials in which researchers have compared "real" acupuncture (in which the needles are inserted according to traditional theory) and "sham" acupuncture (in which the needles are inserted at spots that lack therapeutic utility, according to Chinese philosophy), no difference in effectiveness has generally been found.

ACUPUNCTURE AND HORSES

Supporters of acupuncture occasionally refer to studies of the treatment's effects on animals, claiming that they clearly demonstrate an analgesic effect. For example, some researchers have concluded that acupuncture needles can produce sufficient anesthetic effect to enable them to perform midline abdominal incisions on dogs and cats (similar research has yet to be conducted on horses). Advocates of acupuncture conclude that, because animals aren't prone to suggestion, there's no possibility of a placebo effect.

HORSES, HISTORY AND ACUPUNCTURE

Do ancient Chinese bas-reliefs (rock carvings) contain evidence that warriors used "arrow acupuncture" on their horses to prepare them for battle? Several proponents of veterinary acupuncture say yes, but it's worth a closer look.

The bas-reliefs in question are displayed in the Chinese Rotunda at the University of Pennsylvania's Museum of Archaeology and Anthropology in Philadelphia. The Museum's Web site contains a color illustration and the following description:

The two bas-reliefs of horses (circa a.d. 618–906) on the rotunda's west wall were two of six reliefs commissioned by Emperor T'ai-tsung, founder of the T'ang Dynasty, for his mausoleum. The portraits of the six favorite horses T'ai-tsung had ridden in his battles to secure the empire's borders are well-known in Chinese history and literature. Each horse is identified by the position of its arrow wound. The pictured relief shows General Ch'iu

Hsing-kung, who had given up his own unwounded horse to the
Emperor, pulling an arrow from the chest of Autumn Dew, the
Emperor's wounded charger.

Other factors may be playing a part in the apparent success ᴏ
acupuncture in animals, however. Animals must be restrained fᴏ
acupuncture treatment as well as for surgery. Restrained animᴀ
can appear to be anesthetized as a result of fear and catalepsy (tʜ
so-called "still reaction"). And "real" and "sham" acupuncture hᴀ
not been compared in animal studies.

Early studies suggested that acupuncture might help relieve bᴀ
pain in horses, and nonrandomized, uncontrolled trials appeaɪ
to support this hypothesis. But one of the very few randomiᴢ
clinical trials of acupuncture in horses with lower-limb arthr
showed that horses treated with acupuncture fared no better tʜ
untreated controls. In addition, there is no evidence to suggest t
acupuncture helps in treating colic, chronic obstructive pulmon
disease or reproductive disorders. In general, the same problᴇ
that beset human acupuncture studies—namely, the lack of ef
under controlled conditions—appear to be present in equine stu
as well.

SAFETY ISSUES

Acupuncture is not without its risks. Complications from
puncture needles—even fatal ones—have been described in hu
medicine, although they do not appear to be particularly comɪ
Reports of direct adverse effects in horses from acupunᴄ

treatment have not been described. In 1998, a California handler who was injured during a horse's electro-acupuncture treatment received a large settlement. Because acupuncture involves puncturing the skin, it should be regarded as a surgical procedure; good surgical technique, including preparation of needle sites, sterile needles and gloved hands, is a must.

DIFFUSE NOXIOUS STIMULUS

The concept of a diffuse noxious stimulus is well-recognized in neurophysiology. It's well known that a painful or uncomfortable stimulus at one point can decrease pain perception at another (if you have a headache and someone kicks you in the shin, your head may not hurt as badly). Might this be the cause of some of the reported effects of needling?

ASSESSING ACUPUNCTURE: THE CRUCIAL QUESTIONS

Acupuncture's apparent benefits are primarily anecdotal, but to assess the modality properly its objective value must be quantified. To be able to ascribe any benefit to the therapy, one must first exclude the disease's natural history and the placebo effect. There must be clear evidence of a distinction between general counter-irritant techniques, which may offer mild pain relief, and acupuncture. In addition, there must be evidence that inserting

needles at random points does not produce the same effect as specific needling.

Before traditional Chinese acupuncture can be proven effective, researchers must know which version and which acupoints are being tested and why. Scientific journals do everyone a disservice when they fail to provide this information.

IMPLICATIONS FOR THE HORSE OWNER

Modern science has so far failed to provide supportive evidence for acupuncture's claims of producing a therapeutic effect through the insertion of needles at particular points on the body. The claims of many acupuncturists and acupuncture organizations generally are not supported by clinical-research findings. Until such time as supporting evidence becomes available, acupuncture should not be offered without full informed consent. Clients must be advised of the therapy's unproven status, its possible adverse effects and the availability of less-invasive, equally effective alternatives.

STEPHEN BASSER

Stephen Basser received his M.B., B.S. (Bachelor of Medicine, Bachelor of Surgery—the Australian equivalent of an M.D.) from Melbourne University. He has worked in general practice (the equivalent of family medicine in the United States) since 1996. He has written papers for the Australian Skeptics on acupuncture, chiropractic, the anti-immunization movement and therapeutic-goods legislation.

JACK RASO

Jack Raso, M.S., R.D., earned a B.S. in nutrition and dietetics from the Pratt Institute in Brooklyn, New York and a M.S. in health science from Long Island University in Brooklyn. He is the director of publications at the American Council on Science and Health and the editor-in-chief of its quarterly, *Priorities for Health*, a contributing editor to the *Scientific Review of Alternative Medicine* and the author of several books, including *"Alternative" Healthcare: A Comprehensive Guide*.

WALLACE SAMPSON

Dr. Wallace Sampson is board-certified in internal medicine and is a Fellow of the American College of Physicians. He is a clinical professor of medicine at Stanford University School of Medicine, where for 20 years he has taught the analysis of dubious medical claims. He is a Fellow of the Committee for the Scientific Investigation of Claims of the Paranormal and editor-in-chief of the *Scientific Review of Alternative Medicine*.

CHAPTER EIGHT

Manual Therapy: Chiropractic

with Joseph Keating, Ph.D.

Chiropractic is the brainchild of Daniel David Palmer, a native of Canada who immigrated to the American Midwest in 1865. A dabbler in metaphysical approaches to health care, he reported that a spiritual medium inspired him in his search for "the [single] cause of all disease." In 1886, he established a clinical practice as a magnetic healer, and he eventually developed a 40-bed inpatient facility.

While practicing in Davenport, Iowa in 1896, Palmer developed a theory that all disease is caused by spinal *subluxations*, or misaligned vertebrae. He postulated that subluxations produced pressure on nerves, which then caused excesses or deficiencies in various bodily functions. Manipulating the vertebrae to realign the spine, he theorized, would free the nerves, and the problems would disappear.

In 1896, a local minister named Palmer's new theory by combining the Greek words *cheir* (hands) and *praxis* (act or action) to form a new word, *chiropractic*. That same year, Palmer founded

Palmer's School of Magnetic Cure, which was renamed the Palmer School and Infirmary of Chiropractic in 1907. It took its current name, the Palmer College of Chiropractic, in 1961. The Palmer College has graduated thousands of chiropractors, and today chiropractic is the most widely used alternative treatment method in the United States.

A HISTORY OF MANUAL THERAPY

Although Palmer is considered the father of modern chiropractic, he did not invent the technique of manipulation, nor are chiropractors the only practitioners to use it. Many forms of manual therapy are found in native cultures around the globe. For hundreds of years, British folk practitioners called *bonesetters* have suggested that when bones "go out of place," various painful maladies can result. Most bonesetters taught their craft to their children, thereby keeping it a family secret.

Although European and early American bonesetters tended to limit their craft to relieving muscular disorders (such as aches, pains and dislocations), Palmer asserted that his methods could cure a much wider range of ills. Like his contemporary, Andrew Taylor Still, the founder of osteopathy, Palmer believed that he could relieve all or most of his patients' "dis-ease" by using only his hands to reposition their body parts. (Osteopathy, known today as osteopathic medicine, gradually abandoned its commitment to Still's theories and embraced the scientific method.)

Today, physiotherapists, athletic trainers and several types of medical doctors employ manipulation and mobilization techniques and other manual therapies to treat various conditions that affect nerves, joints and muscles. Also referred to as musculoskeletal medicine, manual therapies are (as the name suggests) hands-on procedures used in an attempt to help restore normal movement by moving joints and stretching tight muscles. When a joint is stretched a little beyond its normal range of motion, you'll often hear a popping or a cracking sound (the same sound you get when you crack your knuckles). Whether the popping sound has any clinical meaning from a therapeutic point of view isn't known. The technique of mobilization stretches soft tissues by taking joints through a full range of movement.

CHIROPRACTIC PHILOSOPHY EXAMINED

The subluxation is not only the theoretical basis of chiropractic but its legal foundation as well. Many state laws describe chiropractic as the finding and removing of subluxations. Yet to this day, no definitive evidence of the clinical meaningfulness of subluxations exists; and in carefully designed studies, chiropractors themselves have been unable to agree on the presence or absence of subluxations.

Because of this lack of a scientific basis and despite gains in popularity and in legal standing, chiropractic remains controversial.[1] The College of Physicians and Surgeons of the Province of Quebec published a critique of chiropractic in 1963, and it's still apt. It states:[2]

Chiropractors claim that subluxations, or partial displacements, of the vertebrae cause a perturbation of the distribution of nervous impulses to tissues and cells. Neurophysiologists have developed methods of recording the passage of impulses in nerves. . . . No scientific study has ever been published on the subject by a chiropractor. No chiropractor ever defined, either quantitatively or qualitatively, what chiropractic means by perturbation of nervous impulses. Is it their number, their amplitude, their frequency or their wave patterns which are affected? All of these qualities can be identified, recorded and studied. It is no longer permissible to accept empirical statements . . .

The little research that has been done outside the chiropractic profession has not been favorable. In 1973, Yale University anatomist Edmund Crelin, Ph.D., demonstrated in human cadavers that it was impossible to produce joint misalignments severe enough to pinch the nerves that lie between the spinal bones without destroying the spine.[3] Manual therapy still may have its benefits, but the theory on which the entire field is based is suspect. Chiropractors have only recently begun to try to identify the conditions that might be amenable to chiropractic therapy and which adjustment methods should (and should not) be used in each one.[4]

CHIRO CONTROVERSY

More than 100 more-or-less distinct methods of spinal correction exist in human chiropractic. Some chiropractors believe in adjusting only the first vertebra, the *atlas*. Others believe that only the *sacral* area (the lower end of the spine) is important. Still others adjust both ends (for example, in the sacro-occipital technique).

Some chiropractic theories state that each vertebra affects different organs and thus is related to different diseases.

Chiropractors may measure leg lengths, search for abnormal spinal-heat patterns or employ elaborate X-ray marking systems in an effort to detect subluxations. Some practitioners test patients' muscles, even looking for weakness or strength in muscles that, they assert, are associated with certain foods, colors, music and other factors (a practice known as applied kinesiology).

Chiropractors also disagree about the scope of their methods. Some favor limiting the practice to manual manipulations of the spine; others say that all joints can benefit from manual therapy. Some chiropractors use soft-tissue techniques and physiotherapeutic modalities (such as heat, electricity and traction), recommend therapeutic exercises, make suggestions about diet, employ psychological/behavioral techniques or prescribe dietary supplements and vitamins. Some of these methods have been shown to be effective in disciplines apart from chiropractic, but the effects and value of the unique combinations used by some chiropractors are largely untested.

The U.S. Department of Health and Human Services' Office of the Inspector General addressed the confusion about subluxations, the scope of chiropractic practice and other important health-care issues in a 1986 report, which stated in part that "There continues to be some disagreement within the profession regarding which conditions are appropriate for chiropractic care and regarding appropriate parameters for treatment." The report went on to assert that ". . . there also exist patterns of activity and practice which at best appear as overly aggressive marketing and, in some cases, seem deliberately aimed at misleading patients and the public regarding the efficacy of chiropractic care."

A very few chiropractors publicly acknowledge their skepticism about subluxations.[5] They offer their skills as manipulation therapists only when they believe that such treatment is clinically justified and are happy to refer patients to other health-care providers. A few work in association with medical physicians and surgeons, although what percentage of chiropractors fit this description is unknown. A few chiropractic colleges are actively involved in scientific research, but others perpetuate anti-scientific attitudes among students and the field.[6]

Chiropractic Consumer Advocates

Is there a science of chiropractic? One organization is trying to establish one: The National Association for Chiropractic Medicine (NACM), a consumer-advocacy association of chiropractors who confine their scope of practice to established boundaries.

NACM members must be doctors of chiropractic (D.C.) who renounce traditional chiropractic philosophy—theories that as yet have no scientific validity. For more information, visit the NACM's Web site: www.chiromed.org.

IS CHIROPRACTIC A PLACEBO?

Despite chiropractic's limited scientific validation, it has a loyal client following. Some of its popularity may result from its potent psychological components. In his book *Bonesetting, Chiropractic and Cultism*, reformist Samuel Homola, D.C., writes:

> *The majority of the "subluxations" commonly found by many chiropractors are likely to be painless and imaginary. . . . [the] thrust [of the chiropractor's hands], with "popping" of the vertebrae, has a tremendous psychological influence over the mind of the healthy patient as well as over the mind of the sick patient.*

Psychological, suggestive or placebo effects are present in practically every form of health care and are not inherently undesirable. But if you ignore the potential for placebo effects, you may draw incorrect conclusions about a remedy's effectiveness.

Some studies have indicated that chiropractors are better at satisfying their patients than medical doctors.[7] Perhaps chiropractors validate problems that medical doctors or veterinarians tend to minimize. Perhaps the more simplistic explanations about health and disease that they may offer are more accessible or understandable. Perhaps chiropractors just work harder at being friendly. They also offer both a mechanistic and a metaphysical (spiritual) explanation for the apparently beneficial effects of their art, thereby appealing to both needs.

EQUINE CHIROPRACTIC

Palmer developed his methods for use on humans, but the archives of the Palmer Chiropractic Museum in Iowa contain a diploma that was created for equine adjusters. However, no evidence exists that a course in equine spinal manipulation was ever taught or that any such diplomas were issued. No formal attempts to apply chiropractic theories to horses (or any other animals) appear to have taken place until the American Veterinary Chiropractic Association (AVCA) was formed in the 1980s.

Despite the existence of the AVCA, no evidence exists that chiropractic is useful in treating any equine condition, and the unproven and discredited subluxation theory appears to be prominent among equine manual-therapy practitioners. In her chapter on "Chiropractic" in the book *Healing Your Horse* (New York: Howell Book House, 1993), Sharon Willoughby, D.V.M., D.C., writes, "A subluxation can be defined as a misaligned vertebra that is 'stuck' or unable to move correctly and is causing pressure on nerves." Because subluxations and misaligned vertebrae have not been shown to exist, this assertion is not scientifically supported.

She goes on to say, "Since the nervous system integrates and controls the functions of all the tissues and cells, there must be undisturbed nerve transmission in both directions for the body to function properly." This statement is incorrect. Any number of tissues, including the heart, the lungs, the kidneys and the liver, can function just fine without any connection to the nervous system whatsoever.

"Subluxations have been incriminated in decreased or asymmetrical sweating patterns, changes in estrus cycles and chronic abdominal pain," according to Willoughby. No scientific substantiation for this assertion exists in the veterinary or medical literature, however. Despite the lack of supporting evidence, Willoughby attributes a great many equine afflictions to subluxations: "abnormal posture, discomfort when saddling, discomfort when riding, wringing tail, pinning ears, grinding teeth, refusal or unwillingness over jumps, development of unusual behavior patterns, sensitivity to touch, bad attitude, biting, unfriendliness, unusual, perhaps indefinable gait abnormalities, stiffness, obscure lameness . . . " Apparently no condition cannot be caused by a subluxation, yet the clinical usefulness of equine spinal manipulation has not been demonstrated.

Willoughby continues, "The purpose of an adjustment is to realign the spine." No one has shown that the equine spine can even go out of alignment. Although manipulation may have value for reasons that have nothing to do with subluxations, the issue, from a scientific standpoint, is that you can't honestly say that you're treating something if you can't show that it exists.

EQUINE CHIROPRACTORS' QUALIFICATIONS

In most states, the practice of chiropractic is, by definition, restricted to humans. Formal doctoral programs in chiropractic deal exclusively with the treatment of people. A veterinarian's education does not include manipulative physiotherapies. So who exactly is adjusting horses, anyway?

Adjusters include some doctors of chiropractic (D.C.'s) and some veterinarians. A few D.C.'s are also licensed veterinarians. There also appear to be many self-proclaimed animal chiropractors who are neither veterinarians nor chiropractors.

The AVCA certifies veterinarians and D.C.'s after 150 hours of education and also offers advanced courses. The idea that 150 hours is sufficient for an education in chiropractic or veterinary medicine may be surprising, in light of the fact that it takes four years to earn a degree in either field. To be fair, the AVCA asserts that its certification is just the beginning of a chiropractic education.

If you think 150 hours of education isn't much, you may be shocked to learn that some organizations offer one-day seminars on the subject! Either animal chiropractic is so easy that anyone can do it with a minimum of training, or something fishy is going on.

LEGAL ASPECTS OF EQUINE CHIROPRACTIC

Most states restrict the practice of animal chiropractic to veterinarians. According to law, D.C.'s may work on animals under direct veterinary supervision. In this situation, D.C.'s are working as unlicensed veterinary technicians. Any practitioner who is neither a licensed veterinarian nor working under a vet's supervision is probably breaking the law.

MECHANICAL ASPECTS OF EQUINE CHIROPRACTIC

It should be obvious that the forces on the spine of a four-legged animal are quite different from those on the spine of a two-legged human. It follows, then, that chiropractic theories and practices that were developed for use in humans may not apply to animals.

Is it even possible to adjust a horse? Equine vertebrae are the size of your fist or larger and covered on all sides by thick, tough layers of muscle, tendon and ligament that are several inches thick. How can the human hand possibly apply enough force to significantly affect a horse's vertebrae? Yet proponents of equine chiropractic assert that the technique requires almost no force at all to do so.

WHAT DOES CHIROPRACTIC MANIPULATION REALLY DO?

When chiropractors are challenged to explain precisely what effect nerve impingement has on nerve impulses, they have difficulty coming up with a plausible answer. Instead of giving specifics, they may offer one or more of the following:

"We don't know how it works, but it does." Not true: In horses, as in humans, no one knows which (if any) methods work or for which patients or for which problems.

"Studies to determine the mechanism are under way or just completed but unpublished." This assertion may or may not be true, but allegedly forthcoming evidence doesn't constitute proof.

"Pathological processes may be influenced by disturbances of the nervous system. Disturbances of the nervous system may be the result of derangements of the musculoskeletal structure. Disturbances of the nervous system may cause or aggravate disease in various parts or functions of the body." There are too many 'maybes'! Such statements may be true, but they don't support the subluxation theory or the general notion that spinal problems are an underlying cause of disease.

"Chiropractic is a complementary therapy. Veterinary medicine has its role; we have ours." No one has demonstrated that chiropractic care helps horses.

"Chiropractic focuses on prevention and on helping the body to heal itself." No study has demonstrated that chiropractic care plays any role in preventing disease or promoting healing in horses or humans.

"Chiropractic is not a cure; it can only help to correct any problems that may exist in your horse's spine, thus helping his body to heal itself as best it can." This sort of rhetoric may keep patients coming back, but according to current scientific knowledge, it's unproven.

IS EQUINE CHIROPRACTIC EFFECTIVE?

The veterinary literature does not suggest that chiropractic manipulations have any beneficial effects on horses, but there is considerable literature regarding its application to humans.

Most people see chiropractors for lower-back pain, and lower-back pain is the most frequently studied condition in research on spinal manipulation. The results of the studies are still unclear, although the evidence suggests that manipulation is one of several useful remedies.[8]

However, the data does not suggest that chiropractors' segment-specific thrusting form of manipulation is necessarily better in treating back pain than are other types of manipulation, exercise or massage. The most reasonable interim conclusion about chiropractic manipulation as a treatment for lower back pain in humans is that it may help in some cases, but that its effectiveness has not been absolutely established.

Spinal manipulation also is used to relieve some types of human neck pain as well as tension headaches and muscle and joint aches.[9] However, massage may be as effective as cervical manipulation in relieving tension headaches, and physical therapy may be as effective as spinal manipulation in relieving back pain. There is no evidence that spinal manipulation helps conditions that are not related to the musculoskeletal system.

IS EQUINE CHIROPRACTIC SAFE?

Injuries to horses from overly aggressive manipulations have been reported in lay publications as well as by veterinarians. In humans, manipulations of the neck have caused severe adverse reactions, such as tearing of the internal arteries (and death) and paralysis resulting from fractures. These sorts of reactions are not common—they range from I per 200,000 to one per million cervical manipulations—but they do occur. Manipulating the neck of a horse with an injured or deformed vertebra carries the risk of severe and permanent harm to the spinal cord. Taking your horse's limbs past their normal range of motion also is potentially harmful.

If you decide to have an equine chiropractor work on your horse, protect yourself and your horse by doing the following:

1. Obtain a precise diagnosis before you have someone manipulate your horse's spine. If he has a serious injury, spinal manipulation may cause real harm.

2. Be skeptical of a practitioner who attributes any or all of your horse's problems to vertebral subluxations or misaligned bones. Be especially wary of anyone who tells you that nonmusculoskeletal problems (such as allergies and colic) are related to the spine.

3. Avoid any chiropractor who wants to treat your horse on a regular basis for maintenance.

4. Avoid practitioners who suggest that veterinarians are antichiropractic or who imply that chiropractic is superior to veterinary medicine in treating horses.

5. Avoid any practitioner who uses devices to work on your horse. Don't let someone pound on him with a mallet or a two-by-four.

6. Avoid equine chiropractors who suggest that your horse's legs are different lengths. There is no scientific validation that this finding has any meaningful relationship to your animal's health.

7. Avoid anyone who wants to tranquilize or anesthetize your horse before manipulating him. If he's sedated or knocked out, he can't protect himself.

8. Do not use a chiropractor who is not a doctor of veterinary medicine (D.V.M.) or equivalent, who is not working under your veterinarian's direct supervision or who is unwilling to work with your veterinarian.

9. Avoid any equine chiropractor who suggests that you should call him or her first if your horse becomes ill, injured or lame.

IMPLICATIONS FOR THE HORSE OWNER

Even if an equine-chiropractic practitioner possesses useful skills in manipulative therapy, no scientific evidence exists to suggest that your horse will benefit from it. If you do decide to have your horse worked on in this way, make sure that the practitioner works closely with your veterinarian, if they are not one and the same person. Be aware that, if your horse turns out to have a serious condition, going the chiropractic route first may delay his getting proper treatment at worst and add considerably to your costs at best.

It's easy to see how, through their desire to do the best for their animals, horse owners could be convinced that "People need adjusting, so horses must, too!" No studies have shown that chiropractic adjustment does anything for horses or any other animals.

Moving your horse's limbs around, massaging his muscles or giving him any sort of attention may make him (and you) feel good, but no proof exists that such ministrations are in any way therapeutic.

JOSEPH KEATING

Joseph Keating holds a Ph.D. from the State University of New York at Albany. He is a professor at the Los Angeles College of Chiropractic, where he teaches "History of Chiropractic" and "Philosophy and Reasoning." In 1987, he co-founded the National Institute of Chiropractic Research. Dr. Keating serves on the editorial board of several blind, peer-reviewed journals and is the author of several hundred professional papers and the books *B.J. of Davenport: The Early Years of Chiropractic*, *A History of Chiropractic Education in North America* and *Toward a Philosophy of the Science of Chiropractic: A Primer for Clinicians*.

NOTES

1. Kaptchuk, T. J., and Eisenberg, D. M. "Chiropractic: Origins, Controversies and Contributions." *Archives of Internal Medicine* 158 (1998): 2215–24.

2. Crelin, E. "A Scientific Test of the Chiropractic Theory." *Scientific American* 61 (1973): 574–80.

3. Haldeman, S., Chapman-Smith, C., and Petersen, D. M., editors. *Guidelines for Chiropractic Quality Assurance and Practice Parameters: Proceedings of the Mercy Center Consensus Conference.* Gaithersburg, MD: Aspen, 1993.

4. Nelson, C. F. "The Subluxation Question." *Journal of Chiropractic Humanities* 7 (1997): 46–55.

5. Seaman, D. "Philosophy and Science Versus Dogmatism in the Practice of Chiropractic." *Journal of Chiropractic Humanities* 8 (1998): 55–66.

6. Keating, J. C. "Chiropractic: Science and Anti-Science and Pseudoscience, Side by Side." *Skeptical Inquirer* 21(4)(1997): 37–43.

7. Cherkin, D. C., and MacCormack, F. A. "Patient Evaluations of Low Back Pain Care from Family Physicians and Chiropractors." *West. J. Med.* 150 (1989): 351–355.

8. Bigos, S. J. et al, editors. *Clinical Practice Guideline No. 14: Acute Lower Back Problems in Adults.* Rockville, MD: Agency for Health Care Policy and Research, 1995.

9. Coulter, I. D. et al, editors. *The Appropriateness of Manipulation and Mobilization of the Cervical Spine.* Santa Monica, CA: RAND, 1996.

CHAPTER NINE

Manual Therapy: Massage

with Peter M. Tiidus, M.Sc., Ph.D., FACSM;
Robert Jan Myran, NCTMB, WI-RMT, CNMT;
and Rochelle Barnes Myran, NCTMB, WI-RMT

Another form of hands-on therapy, massage appears to have
become quite popular in recent years. A number of schools certify
equine massage therapists, there are countless ads and flyers from
people who want to rub your horse and you can find any number
of books and articles on the subject. But is massage more than a
feel-good treatment?

THE HISTORY OF MASSAGE THERAPY

The laying on of hands in an effort to promote healing is one of
the most ancient of healing practices. It is described in the oldest
existing medical work, the Chinese *Nei Ching*, as well as in ancient
Indian and Greek medical texts. The practice later spread throughout the Roman Empire, but its reputation was tarnished for more
than 1,000 years through its association with that era's decadence.

The word *massage* comes from the French verb *amaser* (to knead, as
in bread dough). It appears to have been first revived in Europe by
French colonists who witnessed the technique in India in 1779.
The practice of modern massage began in 1863 with the publication

of a French treatise, *Du Massage*, which classified the various techniques according to which bodily system each was supposed to affect. This classification sparked further development of contemporary massage techniques.

WHAT IS MASSAGE?

On the simplest level, massage is the application of pressure to muscles, joints and various other tissues. Although the pressure is commonly applied with the hands, any number of other methods have been devised, from walking on people's backs to the use of vibrating devices.

Modern massage techniques include the following:

- *Effluerage:* Slow, rhythmic stroking motions along the lines of the muscle fibers.

- *Compression:* Slow, circular compressions of the soft tissues against the bones underneath. In a variant of compression known as *jostling*, which is performed on horses, the practitioner lays his or her hands over the withers with the thumbs on the side of the neck he or she is standing on and fingers on the other side. The therapist pulls the neck while pressing the thumbs into the tissue. The process is repeated every few inches, along the length of the horse's neck.

- *Petrissage:* Although several variations exist, petrissage is generally described as a forceful "milking stroke" that is used only on flesh areas. The practitioner alternately lifts and squeezes the large muscles with both hands in an attempt to stimulate the deeper tissues. Petrissage usually is not used on horses because most equine massage therapists keep one hand on the horse's flank to help guard against kicks.

- *Frictions:* These firm, penetrating, rapid strokes are applied with deep pressure through the fingertips. Usually circular movements, frictions can be applied with or across the muscle fibers or even in a circular fashion.

- *Tapotement:* The therapist tries to vibrate the tissues by tapping or lightly beating on them.

- *Vibrations:* The therapist vibrates his or her hands firmly against the skin.

Many people consider a good massage to be an invigorating and enjoyable pleasure, but despite massage's long history and widespread popularity, it has actually been subjected to relatively little scientific study. As with other areas of alternative medicine, many of the studies that have been conducted failed to use control groups or blinding, used small samples, and even suffered from publication bias (in which positive studies get reported and negative studies don't), rendering their results less than scientifically significant. More recently, though, a number of good studies have provided useful information about both the true benefits of and the false claims that have been made about various massage techniques. All the studies have been conducted on humans or laboratory animals; none has been done on horses. Still, it's worth taking a look at what is known about massage.

MASSAGE AND RELAXATION

Some studies in people suggest that back massages help depressed children and adults to feel better. The technique seems to help reduce biochemical indications of stress and results in reports of more positive moods. As for horses, many seem to enjoy being handled and appear to relax while getting a good rub, even leaning into the therapist's hands or nuzzling him or her during the treatment. In this regard, massage has little potential to cause your horse harm: If the horse doesn't like it, it will probably let you know pretty quickly.

MASSAGE AND MUSCLE KNOTS

Ever have a kink in your neck? Massage therapists often speak of helping to loosen areas of muscle that feel tight or as if they have knots in them. However, no hard data exists on the effectiveness of massage on relaxing muscle knots or even on the existence of muscle knots themselves. Clinical and anecdotal evidence of muscle tightness, cramping, spasms and related pain and discomfort or soreness related to the musculoskeletal system has been documented, though; perhaps some of these conditions could also be described as muscle knots.

Certain types of massage may have some effect in reducing muscle tightness or in producing a general relaxation effect. Although these effects have not been well-documented with empirical evidence, there are numerous anecdotal claims of their effectiveness. This area is another one in which massage appears to have little potential for harm.

MASSAGE AND CIRCULATION

One of the most frequently claimed benefits of massage is that it improves blood circulation to the area being rubbed. There is no question that blood is important; it brings all sorts of good things to the cells and carries away the residue of the body's biochemical work. However, no good evidence exists that increasing circulation via massage is even possible, let alone beneficial.

From the standpoint of basic physiology, one might ask why massage therapy *would* improve circulation. The blood circulation to each tissue is fairly precisely controlled and is determined by that tissue's needs. The tissues generally receive just enough blood to handle their metabolic requirements—no more and no less.

During exercise, working muscles need more blood, and the heart pumps faster to supply that need. If a more active metabolic area (such as the working muscle) requires more blood than the heart can supply, the body shunts blood away from other, less metabolically active areas. (That's why, during long periods of exercise, horses' intestines experience reduced blood flow.) Therefore, massage would not produce a significant circulatory effect unless it increased the muscles' metabolic needs, which is unlikely. Even if massage did increase the muscles' metabolic needs, the heart rate would have to increase to satisfy those needs.

Good experimental evidence from humans shows that the massage of both large and small muscle groups does not affect blood flow to those muscles, either during or after the massage. In other words, the simple application of rhythmic pressure to a muscle will not draw more blood to it. The pressure and friction involved in rubbing or striking the skin might produce temporary flushing or redness (indicating that there is more blood in the capillaries of the skin), but the same effect is unlikely in the underlying muscular tissue. It would be virtually impossible for massage to affect the blood circulation to a horse's enormous muscles.

Of course, there is a way to increase the blood flow to your horse's muscles: exercise. Exercise increases the blood flow up to 20 or 30 times that of resting levels, largely to provide working muscles with the additional nutrients they need to sustain their activity. (Even light exercise, such as walking, greatly elevates the blood flow to working muscles.)

Massage is also purported to affect the lymphatic system, which carries nonblood bodily fluids. A horse with "stocked-up" legs has accumulated excess lymphatic fluid there, and massaging its legs may temporarily help reduce the swelling.

Lymphatic drainage in humans is done slowly and lightly, and the massage takes several hours. Most of the evidence for the effectiveness of massage in the removal of lymphatic fluid shows that massage encourages the removal of fluids directly beneath the skin (subcutaneous fluids). No studies have indicated that massage can affect swelling in deeper tissues, such as muscle.

Other methods of controlling lymphatic swelling in humans include the application of compressive garments, mechanical pumps or even using the principles of gravity (elevating a swollen leg). If your horse's legs get puffy when it's stabled, applying stable bandages can help control the swelling. The bottom line, though, is that, in both humans and horses, light exercise is generally considered to be more effective than massage in eradicating lymphatic swelling.

MASSAGE AND "TOXINS"

The concept of body toxins is common to a variety of alternative therapies. In the early twentieth century, for example, disease was thought to be largely the result of *autointoxication* from bad stuff in the bowels. This idea was the theoretical foundation for a national obsession with daily bowel movements (regularity) and the use of enemas to treat all manner of ailments.

It is true that cellular metabolism, which increases during exercise, produces byproducts (lactic acid and others) that are removed by the bloodstream. As circulation to the working muscles increases during exercise and the post-exercise cool-down period, these byproducts are removed quickly, usually within 30 minutes of stopping the exercise. Studies on humans have shown that light recovery exercise speeds up this process but that massage is no more effective than passive rest in encouraging the removal of the byproducts of exercise.

Another point worth noting here is that lactic acid and other so-called toxins do not cause post-exercise muscle soreness, despite the persistence of this widespread belief. Rather, muscle soreness that follows exercise is caused by natural reactions to muscle damage and the physiological repair processes themselves. Toxins cannot be massaged away to alleviate muscle soreness, not only because massage does not affect their removal via circulation, but also because these toxins do not cause the soreness in the first place.

The idea that exercise-produced toxins could accumulate in your horse's body and poison it certainly might worry you if you didn't know anything about physiology. But if it (or you, for that matter) retained wastes and toxins after exercise, your horse would become very ill or even die. Exercise generally doesn't lead to sickness or death. So, the entire concept of eliminating toxins through massage is irrational and unscientific.

MASSAGE AND POST-EXERCISE RECOVERY OF MUSCLE FUNCTION

There is little scientific evidence that massage has any significant impact on the recovery of muscle function following exercise, either short-term (immediately following exercise) or long-term (which involves muscle-repair processes that occur after intense exercise and that may take more than a week to resolve fully). In humans, experimental evidence indicates that massage does not aid in the recovery of muscle strength and performance following anaerobic or intense exercise; neither does massage appear to significantly or consistently affect the physiological factors associated with the process of muscle-function recovery. Neither delayed-onset muscle soreness (the next-day soreness that may occur after a workout) nor functional recovery from muscle damage appears to be significantly affected by massage.

MASSAGE AND TISSUE HEALING

A small body of evidence indicates that massage may facilitate the healing of connective-tissue injuries, at least in laboratory animals. In one study, rats with injured Achilles' tendons showed improved healing following a technique known as augmented soft-tissue mobilization. In general, however, claims that massage can remove scar tissue and adhesions from tendons and muscles are not supported by scientific evidence.

MASSAGE AND INJURY PREVENTION

No studies have looked at the ability of massage to prevent injuries. It's difficult to imagine by what mechanism massage could prevent injury. By relaxing tight muscles, massage could perhaps reduce the likelihood of further injuries, but that's about it.

MASSAGE AND PERFORMANCE

The medical literature on massage's effects on performance is not at all supportive of the contention that massage helps human athletes perform better. But, as was previously stated, there is a good bit of anecdotal information that massage produces feelings of well-being in humans. What isn't known is whether this feeling influences performance. Massage doesn't appear to do any harm, so its continued use may not be inappropriate, as long as you realize that it may not be having any real beneficial effect.

Some equine massage therapists have made rather remarkable claims about massage's effectiveness in enhancing horses' performance. Massage, some therapists claim, can treat problems including refusal or resistance to pick up leads, head and neck discomfort, shortened stride, hind leg scuffing, improper tracking, hip and shoulder lameness, girthing problems, muscular or "cold" back, loss of performing ability and many others. Again, no scientific evidence exists to support any of these contentions.

Anecdotal reports suggest that massage may have some short-term effects in helping horses who refuse or resist changing leads, become short-strided or scuff their hind limbs as they move. Insofar as those things inhibit a horse's ability to perform, massage may be of some benefit. Some endurance riders, for instance, believe that having massage therapists work on their horses' hamstrings results in improved performance. There have been other reports of horses who refused to turn in the direction opposite a tight muscle along the spine but then could turn with no problem after they were massaged. However, the apparent benefits may be the result of the stretching of the previously uncomfortable muscle, and horse owners may be able to achieve the same result by having their animals do "carrot stretches," in which they entice the horse to stretch left, right and down by holding a carrot in the desired direction.

As for the claims that massage can treat sore backs, the identification of back pain is currently an area of considerable controversy in equine medicine. If you believe that your horse's back is sore, it's conceivable that your concerns will be alleviated if you have it massaged. But in the case of a serious problem, such as an injury to her vertebral column, massage would be less likely to be of benefit. Don't overlook the fact that massage may cause your horse to show relief simply because it responds to the attention. While receiving a massage your horse (and you) may forget what is bothering it. This common element in human pain relief may occur in horses as well.

MASSAGE AND PSEUDOSCIENCE

Many of the claims made for massage certainly bear investigating; others, such as the following, are just plain silly:

- Claims that massage increases the number of red blood cells don't hold water. Red blood cells are manufactured inside the bones, which obviously are not accessible from outside the body, and so massage would have no effect.

- Claims that massage lessens joint inflammation and swelling should be met with a raised eyebrow. If a horse's leg were really inflamed and the horse would allow it to be massaged, rubbing the inflamed area could potentially *increase* inflammation.

- Claims that massage lengthens connective tissue, tendons or ligaments are dubious. In humans, connective tissue fascia can be stretched but not permanently elongated. The lengthening of tendons and ligaments would most likely not be in the best interests of either humans or horses, because these tissues have important functions in preventing excessive joint movement.

- Claims that massage frees muscles are impossible to refute because the concept has no inherent meaning.

IMPLICATIONS FOR THE HORSE OWNER

There are many more questions than answers when it comes to massage therapy. Does massage produce any lasting effects? There's not much reason to think that it would, any more than there would be reason to think that the effects of a single dose of a drug would be lasting. Under what conditions should massage therapy *not* be used? Which massage techniques are most effective in producing the desired effects?

Your horse may appear to enjoy being massaged, and standard techniques are unlikely to cause any harm. But at this time, there's no reason to believe that massage is critical in maintaining its health or boosting its athletic performance. However, before any firm conclusions can be drawn, much more data is needed.

PETER TIIDUS

Dr. Peter Tiidus is an associate professor in the Department of Kinesiology and Physical Education at Wilfrid Laurier University in Waterloo, Ontario, Canada and an adjunct professor in the Department of Kinesiology at the University of Waterloo. He is a

Fellow of the American College of Sports Medicine. His research focuses on the effects of exercise on muscle damage, repair and inflammatory responses and on the physiological effects of antioxidant vitamins, hormones and oxygen radicals on exercise-induced muscle damage, repair and inflammation. He has published nearly forty book chapters and peer-reviewed scientific papers on these topics and has made as many presentations at scientific conferences.

ROB AND ROCHELLE MYRAN

Rob and Rochelle Myran are graduates of the Florida Institute of Massage Therapy (now the Florida College of Natural Health) and members of the American Massage Therapy Association, and they maintain a private massage practice in Wisconsin. Rob Myran sits on the Wisconsin Massage Advisory Committee and volunteers on the Regulation/Legislation Committee of National Certification Board for Therapeutic Massage and Bodywork. He is certified in neu-romuscular massage therapy and has accrued more than 225 hours in the approach.

CHAPTER TEN

Magnetic and Electromagnetic Therapy

with Anthony T. Barker, B.Eng., Ph.D., C.Eng., FIEE, FIPEM

Of the many equine products and therapies available, one of the most popular (if the number of advertisements is any indication) is magnetic therapy. Although beneficial effects of low-level magnetic fields have been claimed since the 1500s, scientists still can't agree as to whether any real effects exist. One thing seems clear, however: Research generally doesn't support the product manufacturers' claims.

THE HISTORY OF MAGNETIC THERAPY

The effects of magnets on biologic processes have been discussed for more than 2,000 years. The idea that magnets could be used to treat disease began in the early sixteenth century with the Swiss physician, philosopher and alchemist Paracelsus, who used them to treat epilepsy, diarrhea and hemorrhage. Magnetic therapy really took off when Franz Mesmer, an Austrian doctor who also helped found the fields of hypnotism and psychoanalysis (and from whose name the word *mesmerize* was coined), opened a magnetic-healing salon in Paris in 1777 to treat the untoward effects of the body's innate animal magnetism.

Over the next couple of centuries, magnetic therapy developed into the worst form of quackery. In 1799, Elisha Perkins, a Connecticut physician and sometime mule-trader, began advocating the use of *metallic tractors*, which were small metal magnetic wedges, for the treatment of various ailments in people and horses. The user had merely to sweep the tractors over the injured area for a few minutes to "draw off the noxious electrical fluid that lay at the foot of suffering." Experts and users supplied glowing testimonials, and Perkins became very rich.

The Sears catalog offered magnetic boot inserts in the late 1800s. Thacher's Chicago Magnetic Company hawked a full line of mail-order magnetic caps and clothing—more than 700 magnets in total. Dr. Thacher asserted that "magnetism properly applied will cure every curable disease no matter what the cause." By World War II, however, magnetic fields were no longer receiving much attention in academic medical journals.

All of this history of magnetic quackery has obscured the fact that there has been a great deal of relatively recent medical investigation as to the effects of magnetic and electromagnetic fields on bodily tissues. From a biophysics standpoint, it's very important to separate the two therapies: Magnetic does not equal electromagnetic.

ELECTRICITY AND MAGNETISM

In 1821 the Danish scientist Christian Oersted, who was delivering a lecture in Copenhagen, made the chance observation that passing a current down a wire caused a magnetic field to be generated. Electromagnetic induction was first discovered in 1831 by the English physicist Michael Faraday. (Faraday's discovery led directly to the development of the generator and the transformer and made possible the widespread use of electricity.) He found that running an electric current through a wire coil generated a magnetic field; conversely, he also found that passing a changing magnetic field (one in which the field levels are not constant) through a coil generates an electric voltage in that coil. The magnetic field must change with time to have any electrical effect, hence the term *pulsating electromagnetic field* (PEMF) therapy.

Most experts believe that PEMF therapy's biological effects (if there are any) are electrical, not magnetic. However, a static magnetic field (that is, one that doesn't change) cannot generate electrical voltage; therefore, any effects of a static magnetic field on bodily tissue cannot be electrical. (The magnetic boots and blankets sold for use on horses are static magnetic devices.)

PULSATING ELECTROMAGNETIC FIELD THERAPY

Any number of biological processes respond to mechanical and electrical stimuli in laboratory experiments. Although such stimuli exist in horses, the precise nature of the electromechanical signal is not known. For example, mechanical and electrical signals may help control bone synthesis. In soft tissue, high-intensity, alternating-current electrical fields have been shown to cause changes in cell membranes. However, the theory that electrical signals transfer information to cells remains unproven.

113

Electrical activity takes place in your horse's body all the time. The heart produces electrical currents as it beats, bones produce electrical activity when they're compressed and its system produces electrical activity in the vicinity of wounds. Knowing this, some people have theorized that applying electrical current, either directly (through the application of electric wires) or indirectly (via the effects of a magnetic field), may affect bodily tissues.

In human medicine, electromagnetic field therapy has been most widely studied as a possible means of speeding the healing of bone fractures. A number of studies have suggested that electrical fields generated by electromagnetic field therapy stimulate biologic processes related to bone formation. (At least one study, however, shows that the application of electromagnetic fields delays the healing of fresh fractures.)

ELECTROMAGNETIC FIELDS: HELP OR HAZARD?

Although some people sing the praises of electromagnetic devices as therapy, others fear that electromagnetic fields cause cancer, particularly in people who live near electrical power lines. Their concern isn't shared by a number of major research groups, including the National Cancer Institute and the National Research Council, which point out that the electromagnetic fields produced by power lines are small, that there is no mechanism by which the fields should cause cancer and that existing studies that suggest a link between electromagnetic fields and cancer are flawed.

Other studies suggest that electromagnetic therapy may help promote nerve regrowth and healing of chronic wounds and other soft-tissue injuries. It also may be useful in pain management.

Still, much conflicting information exists. In one study, in which researchers caused experimental inflammation of rats' Achilles tendons, electromagnetic stimulation appeared to provide some initial benefit, but all treated groups were equal to the control groups by day fourteen. Electromagnetic therapy may have limited benefit to injured tendons, perhaps in part because these tissues appear to lack electrical activity.

Furthermore, many studies on electromagnetic fields are flawed. Some were poorly designed, some failed to include independent trials to confirm magnetic-product manufacturers' positive results and some used electrical fields that are much weaker than needed to affect the naturally occurring fields that exist across biological membranes.

Even proponents of PEMF therapy concede that more research must be conducted before this modality can be widely recommended. Advocates still are unable to explain why such relatively weak fields should have biological effects.

STATIC MAGNETIC FIELD THERAPY

The makers of magnetic boots, blankets and pads for horses claim their products produce a variety of healthful effects—effects that are almost completely unsupported by scientific evidence. One such claim is that magnets increase local blood circulation. Blood (indeed, all bodily tissues) contains electrically charged particles called ions. A physics principle known as Faraday's Law states that magnetic fields will exert a force on electrically charged particles, which are a moving current of these ions. An extension of Faraday's Law, called the Hall Effect, states that when a magnetic field is placed at a 90-degree angle to the direction of flow of the electric current, it will tend to move and separate the charged ions. The direction in which the ions move depends on the magnetic pole encountered and the polarity of the charge of the ion.

The Hall Effect implies that when a magnet is placed over flowing blood in which ionic charges (such as sodium and chloride, the components of salt) exist, some force will be exerted on the ions, and a small amount of heat will be produced. Magnet proponents would have you believe that ions in the blood go ping-ponging back and forth across the blood vessel, creating currents like those in a flowing river. The combination of the heat, the altered ionic pattern and the currents, they say, causes the blood vessels to dilate and circulation to increase.

The problem with using Faraday's Law and the Hall Effect to try to rationalize the effects of static magnetic pads is that the force applied by the field is almost infinitesimally small, for two reasons: First, the magnetic field being applied to the tissue is extremely weak; second, the flow of the ionic current (the blood) is extremely slow, especially when compared to the flow of electric current. However, it is possible to estimate the forces applied by a weak magnetic field to flowing blood. Calculations by a Yale University professor suggest that the ions might move as much as *20 percent of the diameter of an atom* under a field of the type typically applied by an equine magnetic pad.

But a magnetic field wouldn't be the only force applied to ions in the horse's blood. A horse's body produces a lot of heat, and that heat also moves ions (and other particles), a phenomenon known as Brownian motion. According to calculations, a horse's body heat should cause the ions to move more than 10 million times farther than would the equine magnetic pads.

At least one manufacturer of magnetic pads asserts that its product increases the effect of charge separation because the north and south magnetic poles are alternated during the manufacturing process. There's nothing mysterious about this sort of magnetic-pole arrangement; in fact, it's commonplace in refrigerator magnets. Alternating the poles creates an increased magnetic gradient, which increases the magnets' sticking power. It's sort of funny to talk about the advantages of arranging magnets in this fashion because doing so decreases the magnets' field strength, because the poles tend to cancel each other out. The magnetic field would potentially exert opposite forces on ions flowing through it, but the decrease in magnetic-field strength would lessen the field's potential influence.

Various manufacturers' designs also appear to have no biological significance. One brand's literature states that the pads' concentric circle arrangement increases the likelihood that the magnetic field is applied perpendicular to flowing blood (which would be necessary to maximize the Hall effect). In truth, however, because the smaller blood vessels run randomly throughout the three dimensions of bodily tissue, there can be no preferred arrangement of the magnetic field that favors a perpendicular orientation.

You also may hear that for magnets to work, the "negative pole" has to be facing the tissue. This statement is just silly: Magnets don't have positive and negative poles. They have north-seeking and south-seeking poles, but these designations are purely arbitrary. The words *negative* and *positive* refer to electrical charges, which static magnets don't have and can't create.

One of the biggest problems with magnetic device manufacturers' claims is that their products' magnetic field is often less than the existing magnetic field of the Earth. One investigation into the potential circulatory effects on horse limbs found that, in the pads studied, there was no measurable magnetic field just one centimeter away from the magnet. Past that distance, the field created by the pad was much weaker than the existing magnetic field.

MAGNETIC FIELDS AND BLOOD FLOW

A number of studies have investigated the effects of static magnetic fields on blood flow. One magnetic pad manufacturer commissioned a study that showed an increase in the flow of a concentrated saline solution (which was five times as salty as normal blood) through a thin glass tube that was exposed to a magnetic field. (And, of course, a glass tube can't dilate the way a blood vessel can.) Dr. George Pratt, professor of electrical engineering at the Massachusetts Institute of Technology, who conducted the study, stated, "Yes, we did some experiments with them [magnetic pads] on a saline solution; they did seem increase the flow of saline through a glass tube. I think it's a long extrapolation to say that the experiments . . . have anything to do with blood. . . . I wouldn't count on curing anybody with those pads."

A second study, commissioned by another magnetic pad manufacturer, evaluated the pads' effects using nuclear scintigraphy, a technique that is useful in identifying areas of blood-vessel dilation and inflammation. That study concluded that magnetic pads caused a "highly significant" increase in blood flow under the pads. The manufacturer has widely touted this study as confirming that the pads promote circulation.

This study is open to criticism on a number of fronts. Most telling, a similar independent study in horses was unable to reproduce the findings. The original study also can be criticized on technical grounds, primarily because of an inaccurate method of evaluation and poor controls.

Numerous other studies of magnetic pads and humans, mice, rats, and horses all have failed to show any effect of magnetic fields on blood circulation. Practically speaking, if a magnet did increase local circulation, you'd expect the area under the magnet to feel warm or redden as a result; but have you ever seen such a thing or heard anyone mention it? You'd also expect strong magnetic fields to produce greater circulatory effects, but no such effects have ever been reported in magnetic resonance imaging (MRI) machines, which generate magnetic forces thousands of times greater than those produced by magnetic pads.

The data leads one to conclude that, at the least, if static magnetic fields do affect bodily tissues, how they produce that effect is unknown. One study has shown that magnetic therapeutic devices produce a strong placebo effect in humans, and the same kind of effect could be at work on horse owners. Equine magnetic boots, blankets and bandages may insulate and retain heat, but that effect is produced by the material, not by the magnets.

MAGNETIC FIELDS AND PAIN RELIEF

Static and PEMF therapy also have been promoted as methods of pain relief. As with magnetic devices' other supposed effects, there is no proof of low-intensity magnetic fields' effects on the nerves that sense pain.

Studies conducted to evaluate the effects of PEMF on pain have produced conflicting results. PEMF therapy has reportedly provided pain relief in the treatment of osteoarthritis of the human knee and cervical spine, persistent neck pain and previously unresponsive chronic pelvic pain in women. However, electromagnetic therapy did not relieve the pain of shoulder arthritis; and a 1994 summary of published trials of nonmedicinal and noninvasive therapies for hip and knee osteoarthritis concluded that there wasn't enough data available to draw any conclusions on the therapy's effectiveness. Another study suggested that magnetic treatment caused an *increase* in human tooth pain.

Poorly controlled Japanese studies indicated that static magnetic devices were highly effective in alleviating subjective symptoms such as neck, shoulder and other muscular pain. One controlled, double-blind pilot study suggested that magnetic pads were effective in relieving myofascial or arthriticlike pain in postpolio syndrome, although every patient in the study, whether being treated with a placebo or a magnet, showed relief from pain. Another study suggested that magnets relieve the foot pain associated with diabetes; other studies concluded that a magnetic foil offered no advantage over plain insoles in treating heel pain and that a magnetic necklace had no effect on neck and shoulder pain. It has also been shown that a strong placebo effect is at work in the perception of pain relief offered by static magnetic devices.

CLINICAL APPLICATIONS OF MAGNETIC FIELDS IN HORSES

Horses receive electromagnetic therapy through boots or blankets and static magnetic therapy via magnetic pads. The latter is considerably less expensive than an electromagnetic machine, and it's easy to apply. Unfortunately, neither form of therapy has been proven to be effective. In studies, daily electromagnetic therapy did increase the concentration of blood vessels in surgically created defects of the equine superficial digital flexor tendon; but as the repair tissue matured and changed, healing appeared to be delayed by the treatment in samples collected at eight to twelve weeks after surgery. No benefit could be demonstrated in the healing of freshly created bone injuries treated with PEMF therapy when compared to untreated control limbs, although another study did suggest an increase in bone activity under electromagnetic field treatment when holes were drilled in equine cannon bones. PEMF therapy had little effect on the metabolism of normal horse bone in another study.

BUYER BEWARE!

Despite hundreds of years of experience and investigation, the state of the art in magnetic therapy appears to have advanced little since the days of Franz Mesmer. Some magnetic product manufacturers' claims sound impressive—until you learn what they're really saying. For example:

- One advertisement reads, "Leading scientists agree that unipolar magnets are superior to bipolar." The leading scientists are not identified. Also, the discovery of a unipolar magnet or magnetic monopole would lead to an almost immediate Nobel prize, because magnetic monopoles have not been shown to exist.

- One company advertises "Tectonic" magnets: Tectonics is a geologic term referring to the study of the earth's structural features.

- One company warns about the side effects of taking "too many pills" and states that "Using . . . magnets means you are not putting anything into your stomach that might cause upset or damage." Another company describes its magnets as "natural as nature" and "wholistic [sic]." Such statements beg the question of whether the devices work.

- One company states that various university studies have "proven" that static magnets increase blood flow, a claim that is contrary to the scientific evidence.

IMPLICATIONS FOR THE HORSE OWNER

If your horse gets hurt, you want the injured tissue returned to full normal function as quickly as possible. Any medical therapy that could be demonstrated to speed healing or promote a recovery to pre-injury strength and resiliency would be extremely valuable. However, as you know, assessing a therapy's effectiveness is problematic. To make matters worse, you're often presented with dubious but persuasive claims that are couched in scientific terms.

Claims that magnetic fields increase circulation, reduce inflammation or speed recovery from injuries are simplistic and unsupported by the weight of experimental evidence. The effects of magnetic fields on bodily tissues are complex, poorly understood and likely to be of little or no biological significance. Although existing magnetic therapies may be harmless, that does not mean that they are worth a try.

ANTHONY T. BARKER

Dr. Anthony T. Barker holds a Ph.D. in medical electronics from the University of Sheffield, England. He is a chartered engineer and member of the Institute of Electrical Engineers and a Fellow in the Institute of Physics and Engineering in Medicine and the Institution of Electrical Engineers. He is a consulting clinical scientist in the Department of Medical Physics and Clinical Engineering at the Royal Hallamshire Hospital in Sheffield, where he also serves as an honorary lecturer.

Dr. Barker's main research interests are the electrical activity of biological systems and their interactions with electromagnetic fields, particularly as they relate to the human body; and he has published dozens of articles on these subjects. His interest in communicating scientific and engineering material to a wide audience is reflected in his recent Engineering and Physical Sciences Research Council Award for the Public Understanding of Science.

CHAPTER ELEVEN

Laser and Light Therapy

with Jeffrey R. Basford, M.D., Ph.D.

Laser light (*laser* is an acronym for Light Amplification by Stimulated Emission of Radiation) is created by any one of several devices that transform electromagnetic radiation into one or more similar wavelengths of highly amplified and coherent light: ultraviolet, visible or infrared. High-power lasers (greater than ten watts) have played an important role in medicine and surgery for many years. Less-powerful lasers, whose output is measured in milliwatts instead of watts, have been used since the late 1960s in an attempt to lessen pain and improve wound healing in animals and humans. Lasers for use on horses have been on the market since the 1970s.

HISTORY OF LIGHT THERAPY

The concept of light as therapy existed long before the invention of the laser. The ancient Greeks used sunlight to strengthen and heal. In the Middle Ages, people used sunlight to combat the plague; and by the late nineteenth century, ultraviolet radiation was used to treat cutaneous tuberculosis (scrofula). Today, experts use ultraviolet radiation to kill bacteria and to treat psoriasis in humans.

The earliest investigators of laser therapy used mostly visible lasers, such as helium neon (HeNe), argon, krypton and ruby. Over time, infrared lasers (whose light is invisible to the naked eye), such as gallium arsenide (GaAs) and gallium aluminum arsenide (GaAlAs), became the most widely used in human therapy. In horses, the HeNe devices remain popular, especially in treating wounds and various injuries.

The early lasers used on humans had very low output powers, less than or equal to one milliwatt (mW). Today, most lasers are between 30 and 100 (or more) milliwatts. But as laser powers have increased, treatment times have decreased, meaning that the total energy used has remained at about the same levels established by the early investigators.

Laser therapy (also known as low-intensity laser therapy and low-power laser therapy) owes much of its popularity to clinical trials and research begun in Hungary and the Eastern-bloc countries. Early reports were fragmented and not rigorously scientific, but they caught the attention of Western researchers. Over the years, interest in lasers and light therapy increased.

Today, low-power lasers are used in many parts of the world in an effort to treat musculoskeletal injuries, pain and inflammation. Their acceptance remains mixed in both the medical and veterinary communities, and the U.S. Food and Drug Administration has yet to approve lasers for any clinical application. Lasers are used less in the United States than in Europe and other parts of the world; according to some reports, more than 40 percent of British physical therapy clinics and almost a third of Scandinavian dental clinics use low-power laser therapy.

LASERS REVOLUTIONIZE SURGERY AND TELECOMMUNICATIONS

Lasers may not yet be proven effective in treating soft-tissue injuries, but lasers have made possible several significant advances in surgery and telecommunications. Their potential as a tool in medicine and surgery developed rapidly after Kumar Patel of Bell Laboratories invented the carbon-dioxide laser in 1964. This device allowed surgeons to both perform intricate operations and stop bleeding using photons instead of scalpels. Today, lasers are inserted inside the body to perform operations that were almost impossible to perform even a few years ago, such as welding detached retinas with shorter (green) lasers. Lasers have certainly revolutionized medicine and surgery, although not necessarily in the way that you might have been led to believe.

With the development in the early 1970s of hair-thin strands of encased glass called *fiber-optic waveguides*, lasers became able to transmit telephone signals. Since then, optical fiber has become telecommunications companies' medium of choice for sending voice, data and video signals.

Once largely electronic, today's telecommunications equipment relies on *photons*, tiny semiconductor lasers that transmit billions of bits of information per second via pulses of light carried over glass fibers. Wavelength division multiplexing technology uses various wavelengths (colors) of light to transmit trillions of bits simultaneously over a single fiber.[1]

HOW DO LASERS WORK?

In order to understand what lasers are supposed to do, you need to know a little bit about how they work. Laser light has three important characteristics that distinguish it from other forms of radiation:

- *Coherency,* which means its light waves are of the same phase.

- *Collimation,* which means the light beam is narrow.

- *Monochromaticity,* which means the light beams are of a pure color.

Coherency and collimation do not appear to be important in terms of lasers' therapeutic value; both the beam shape and the wave phases of laser light are rapidly destroyed as the light beam passes through tissue. What does appear essential is that the light be of a single color; effects seen with one-color light are absent in normal light, with its spectrum of colors.

Laser beams have a unique ability to penetrate deeply into tissue. When you shine light on any surface, one of several things can happen: The light can pass right through; it can bounce off the object it's shined on, with relatively little being absorbed; it can hit the surface and scatter; or it can be absorbed. It stands to reason that for light to be an effective therapy, it must reach the underlying tissues.

To get an idea of how laser therapy might have some effects, you have to do a little math. Research suggests that exposures that deliver tiny amounts of energy, as little as 0.01 Joules/cm², can alter cellular processes. (A *joule* is the international unit of heat; it's equal to one watt per second.) Lasers used in therapy lose about one-third of their energy every 0.5 to 1 millimeter of tissue through which they travel. Because laser-therapy treatments typically involve the delivery of one to four or more J/cm^2, this means that laser light can penetrate six to seven "penetration depths" before its strength drops to below the 0.01 J/cm^2 level. This implies that, depending on its wavelength, laser light can penetrate human tissue to a depth of 0.5 to 2.5 centimeters, meaning that at least some of the light does reach the targeted tissue. Therefore, it seems reasonable to suppose that tissues near the skin surface, such as superficial nerves or some tendons, might respond to laser treatment.

Nobody has yet studied how deeply laser light penetrates equine skin and soft tissues. However, given that equine skin is considerably thicker than human skin and is covered with hair, it is reasonable to surmise that laser light penetrates a horse's skin considerably less deeply.

The strongest support for laser therapy comes from the laboratory. Although some controversy persists, it's been established that laser irradiation does *something* to isolated cells, appearing to alter cellular processes without heating or destroying them. Laser therapy involves such low powers that irradiation can't be detected, and only the smallest of temperature elevations (less than or equal to 0.50 to 0.75° C) is produced.

CLINICAL TRIALS

Whether lasers can be used to effectively treat humans and animals is far less clear. The early reports were anecdotal and tended to be extremely favorable. As research quality improves, legitimate clinical effects are becoming more difficult to find. Proponents of low-level laser therapy continue to advocate its use in treating many soft-tissue, neurological and inflammatory conditions in humans; unfortunately, it's difficult to draw any firm conclusions about its effectiveness. Differences in lasers, techniques, research quality and results make systematic evaluation of laser therapy's benefits difficult. Conditions for which laser therapy is used in human medicine may not have an exact counterpart in the horse, making it even more difficult to draw any conclusions about the effectiveness of equine laser therapy.

WOUND HEALING

Laser therapy first gained prominence after the publication in the late 1960s and early 1970s of reports (from poorly controlled studies, unfortunately) that laser irradiation could heal as many as 70 percent of human lower-extremity skin ulcers that had been unresponsive to other treatments.

Studies of wound-healing in patients are difficult to perform and evaluate. Laboratory and animal studies, which usually are easier to evaluate, offer mixed support for laser therapy's wound-healing properties. Some researchers have found that laser irradiation stimulates the growth of capillaries (tiny blood vessels), increases the formation of granulation tissue, encourages the growth of important structural cells called *fibroblasts* and lessens inflammation. Other researchers have found laser irradiation to enhance, inhibit or have no effect on the function of a variety of microorganisms, cells or a variety of cellular components of the healing process.

Laser irradiation has been reported to speed the healing of chronic wounds in diabetic mice, of experimentally induced teat wounds in dairy cattle and of rats' skin flaps, among others. However, studies in rabbits and rats have found that, although laser irradiation may speed repair in the early stages of wound healing, its effects may be clinically insignificant. Not all studies have produced positive results: Some have found no link between laser irradiation and faster healing in guinea pigs, swine, beagles or rats (in six different studies). It appears that the better the study design is, the less likely it is to produce evidence of an effect.

TENDINITIS

Tendon injuries and inflammation are two of the most widely investigated laser therapy applications. Conventional therapy for both humans and horses (which leaves a lot to be desired) may involve ice, heat, rest, progressive exercise, bandaging or nonsteroidal anti-inflammatory medications (NSAIDs). Unfortunately, none of these approaches produces rapid or consistent benefits.

Initial clinical trials of laser therapy's effectiveness in treating tendinitis in the human shoulder were generally unblinded, uncontrolled and included a variety of diagnoses. As better studies have been performed, the positive effects of laser therapy have tended to disappear. Studies on the treatment of tendinitis in humans generally are unable to distinguish between people who received laser treatment and those who received placebos.

JOINT DISEASE

Rheumatoid arthritis is a common inflammatory disease in humans that affects superficial joints. Even though the condition has never been reported in horses, if laser therapy were to be effective in treating any equine condition, rheumatoid arthritis would appear a good candidate.

Early investigations in humans found that laser therapy lessened pain, swelling, medication use and stiffness; but later controlled studies often found no benefits. One study found that clinical and laboratory signs of rheumatoid arthritis were made worse by low-intensity laser therapy.

Laser therapy appears to be somewhat of a mixed bag in treating the wear-and-tear arthritis (osteoarthritis) that affects both humans and horses. Some studies of humans have reported improved functioning and reduced pain of degenerative arthritis of the jaw and the knee following laser treatment, but controlled and blinded studies fail to show that lasers benefit osteoarthritis of the knee, the thumb and acute ankle sprains. The mixture of lasers, power levels and study designs makes evaluating the effects very difficult.

PAIN RELIEF

Laser therapy in humans is most commonly used to relieve pain. Initial studies in this regard were extremely promising, but the benefits became more subtle and difficult to detect as the studies became more rigorous. As in other studies, laser therapy has produced mixed results in tests of its effectiveness at lessening the pain of conditions ranging from back and mouth problems to tennis elbow and painful "trigger points."

ACUPUNCTURE

Low-intensity lasers have at times been used as "needleless" acupuncture therapy to mixed clinical reviews. Uncontrolled studies typically report that laser acupuncture improved or cured 80 percent or more of the subjects; controlled studies have tended to find the technique either without effect or less beneficial than traditional needle acupuncture.

PROFESSIONAL OPINIONS

In a 1992 survey, more than 500 Dutch health professionals, including dermatologists, physicians, and nurses who worked in nursing homes, were asked to rank a list of treatments for pressure sores on a scale from 0 (harmful) to 10 (excellent). The survey respondents ranked pressure relief and patient education the most highly, from 6.2 to 8.3. They ranked high-protein diets, hydrocolloid dressings and zinc oxide somewhat lower (5.0 to 5.6). Far beneath these methods was laser therapy, which scored a mere 1.5 to 3.1. In a 1994 survey of 200 physicians who specialized in rehabilitative medicine and rheumatology, fewer than 20 percent said they believed laser therapy to be effective in treating musculoskeletal problems.

REVIEWS AND META-ANALYSES

A meta-analysis (a study of studies) of 36 randomized laser therapy studies of human musculoskeletal pain and skin disorders, such as chronic ulcers, was unable to draw any conclusions about laser therapy's effectiveness in treating skin disorders. Despite the fact that the studies reviewed included more than 1,700 subjects in total, the varied study designs and quality levels limited the amount of analysis. Still, the investigators found no clear relationship between the laser dosage applied and the efficacy of therapy.

A focused meta-analysis of 23 trials of musculoskeletal pain in humans found no differences in the effects of active and placebo treatment in studies deemed "adequately blinded" and less than a 10 percent difference in the "insufficiently blinded" subset. The authors concluded that low-level laser therapy has no proven effectiveness in the treatment of musculoskeletal pain. Other reviews have found that there is no particular disease or symptom that appears to respond uniquely to laser therapy, stating that the treatment is "still not an established clinical tool."

LASER THERAPY AND HORSES

There are few reported investigations of the effects of low-intensity laser therapy in horses, and most of the reports that do exist are anecdotal, poorly controlled and unblinded. The differing conditions treated and the different wavelengths and dosages used make it impossible to pool the data and look at the overall picture. As a result, it is difficult to draw firm conclusions on the effectiveness of laser therapy in horses.

In one study, researchers made surgical incisions in horses' skin and superficial digital flexor tendons and treated the incisions with an unnamed low-intensity laser-therapy device. Even examining the incisions under a microscope, the investigators couldn't tell the difference between laser-irradiated and nonirradiated tissue. In addition, a 1999 study was unable to find an effect of laser treatment on the healing of lower limb wounds.

Most of the promotional literature for equine lasers suggests that laser therapy is effective in treating superficial tendon and ligament injuries—an assertion that is not supported by good research. One report of an uncontrolled, unblinded study of forty-two Standardbreds with "chronic bowed tendons" asserted that the treated horses were racing within 120 days of treatment with an infrared 904-nm laser, a remarkable finding indeed. The investigators also stated that two-thirds of the treated horses achieved similar or faster race times and classes than the ones they had prior to the injury.

Another study, which examined a number of factors affecting the clinical outcome of seventy-three National Hunt horses in England with superficial digital flexor tendon injuries, found no statistically significant differences between laser-treated and un-treated horses. In fact, the laser-treated horses tended not to recover as well as the horses that were treated conservatively. Neither of these studies specified the type of lasers and dosages used, nor were the treatments controlled for the severity or duration of the injury.

In one unblinded study, low-intensity laser therapy appeared to promote healing of experimentally induced ulcers of horses' upper air passages. Three poorly defined and unrelated conditions (pharyngeal lymphoid hyperplasia, "check-ligament injuries" and "chronic plantar desmitis") were treated with a 904-nm infrared laser in another uncontrolled study. Based on the percentage of horses that achieved similar or faster race times after treatment, the researchers concluded that the laser therapy was beneficial.

Finally, low-level laser irradiation therapy of acupuncture points of the equine back was described in one study as effective in treating chronic back pain in ten of fourteen horses, based on clinical exams and performance level. Once again, the report was uncontrolled and unblinded, and the improvement occurred over a three-month period, so the possibility exists that the owners' expectations, not the horses' condition, were being treated, or that the problems took care of themselves. In a similar uncontrolled and unblinded study, applying lasers to acupuncture points was deemed as effective as needling or injection in treating horses who had suffered from back pain from 2 to 108 months. It's difficult even to determine whether a horse has back pain, and the problem is further complicated by the fact that the degree of back pain can't be measured.

IS LASER THERAPY SAFE?

The laser beams used in therapy are too weak to damage or destroy tissue. Human patients may experience a brief sensation of warmth or tingling after treatment, but subjects treated with a placebo may report the same sensations. Despite the lack of proven risks, most practitioners avoid using lasers on pregnant women, cancer patients, acute bleeding, growing bone and light-sensitive skin.

Looking directly at the beam of a one-megawatt HeNe (visible red light) beam can give you a headache, according to reports. But if you decide to treat your horse with laser therapy, you risk damaging the back of your eye. To prevent this, wear protective glasses and avoid looking directly at the beam or its reflection (for the same reason that you should avoid looking directly at the sun).

IMPLICATIONS FOR THE HORSE OWNER

Laser therapy has yet to be proven clearly effective in treating humans or horses. Some tantalizing indications of benefits exist, but firm clinical evidence does not. Even in cases that are most likely to benefit from laser therapy, the optimal wavelengths, intensities and dosages have not been determined.

As in several other alternative therapies marketed for use on horses, equine laser devices sell with a variety of unsupported claims. The promotional literature for one such device states that laser therapy can treat such diverse conditions as tendon and ligament injuries, navicular syndrome, arthritis and laminitis ("founder"). The makers of another device claim that their product "automatically" locates acupuncture points—a remarkable claim that has never been put to the test. Advertising claims that lasers "increase blood flow," "re-establish the lymphatic system" or "stimulate endorphins" are simplistic, incomplete and poorly supported by valid research.

On a more positive note, a broad range of laboratory studies has found that laser irradiation can modify cellular processes, and that beam intensities sufficient to produce these effects can indeed be delivered to superficial joints and tissues, at least in humans. The quality of laser-therapy research is improving; but as of this writing, this form of alternative therapy has yet to prove itself more than ineffective at worst and marginally effective at best.

JEFFREY R. BASFORD

Jeffrey R. Basford holds a Ph.D. in experimental physics from the University of Minnesota and an M.D. from the University of Miami. He joined the Department of Physical Medicine and Rehabilitation at the Mayo Clinic in Rochester, Minnesota in 1982. His clinical interests are neurological rehabilitation and musculoskeletal pain. He is the medical director of the department's Hospital Consulting Service, the chair of its Research Committee and a member of its Clinical Practice Executive Committee. He also directs the Mayo Medical Rehabilitation Research Training Grant, which is sponsored by the National Institute of Health.

Dr. Basford has researched stroke and the physiological effects of physical agents on the body. He wrote the "Physical Agents" chapters of most of the physical medicine and rehabilitation textbooks and serves on the editorial boards of the professional journals *Archives of Physical Medicine and Rehabilitation* and *Physical Therapy*.

NOTES

1. Bell Laboratories Web site (www.bell-labs.com/history/laser/). "Schawlow and Townes Invent the Laser." 1999. Used with permission.

CHAPTER TWELVE

Homeopathy

with Mahlon Wagner, Ph.D.

Since it was first proposed as a therapeutic method more than 200 years ago, *homeopathy,* the practice of treating diseases with remedies prepared from extreme dilutions of substances, has fallen in and out of favor. Almost extinct just a few decades ago, homeopathy appears to be enjoying something of a recent resurgence. This chapter looks at the evidence for this very controversial therapy.

HISTORY OF HOMEOPATHY

The German physician Samuel Hahnemann is generally acknowledged to be the founder and developer of homeopathy. Medicine in Hahnemann's time included such barbaric and discredited practices as bleeding, purging, cupping and excessive doses of mercury. Disillusioned, he ceased his medical practice in 1782 and began translating medical and chemical texts. It was during this time that he apparently began to question how the day's popular drugs worked.

Hahnemann agreed with the traditional view of disease as involving the vital force or spirit. He wrote:

> The causes of our maladies cannot be material, since the least foreign material substance, however mild it may appear to us, if introduced into our blood vessels, is promptly ejected by the vital force, as though it were a poison . . . no disease, in a word, is caused by any material substance, but that every one is only and always a peculiar, virtual, dynamic derangement of the health.[1]

According to Hahnemann's philosophy, the symptoms of illness are more important than the external causes. Treatment, then, is a matter of finding the substance or substances that induce the same symptoms in a healthy individual. This theory is the basis of Hahnemann's "Principle of Similars."

PROVING

Hahnemann and his followers tested the effects of almost 100 substances on themselves, a process known as *proving*. A healthy person would ingest a small amount of a substance and then attempt to note any reactions or symptoms (emotional or psychological as well as physical). By this method, they "proved" that the substance was an effective remedy for a particular symptom. Their collected experiences became the basis for a compendium called the *Materia Medica*. (In a later controlled study, healthy subjects reported similar symptoms whether they ingested a homeopathic dilution of belladonna or a placebo.)

POTENTIZATION

Because some of the substances Hahnemann tested were toxic (such as poison ivy, strychnine and various snake venoms), he and his followers would ingest minuscule doses during their proving sessions. This practice may be the source of the homeopathic principle of "infinitesimal dilutions," which alleges that the most dilute solutions are the most potent—another controversial point in this alternative methodology. Believers in "potentization" say that the process activates the diluted, inert substance by releasing its energy. According to Hahnemann,

> *Homeopathic potentizations are processes by which the medicinal properties of drugs, which are in a latent state in the crude substance, are excited and enabled to act spiritually upon the vital forces. You can't just dilute a drug to make it effective. To achieve potentization, after each successive 1:9 (D) or 1:99 (C) dilution, the solution must be shaken vigorously (the process is known as succussion). In the case of a powdered substance, it must be vigorously ground up (trituration).[2]*

HANDLE WITH CARE?

Some proponents of homeopathy state that the remedies can easily lose their effectiveness because of their very special, subtle energy. Consumers may be told to store the remedies far from microwave ovens or electrical appliances, never to open more than one remedy at a time and never to return a pill to the bottle or to transfer the pills to another bottle.

Some practitioners advise their clients to abstain from eating or drinking for at least 30 minutes before taking a dose.

Some homeopaths go so far as to tell clients that simply writing the name of the remedy on a slip of paper and pinning the paper to their pajamas will produce a cure. Some clients have attested to feeling better on the drive home from the homeopath's office, with the remedy nestled safely on the seat beside them. The power of suggestion appears to be alive and well.

Hahnemann believed that homeopathic remedies should be prescribed according to individual body types and personalities, based on the ancient humoral theories of the Greek doctor Galen. Galen postulated that there are four body types and personalities, based on which body humor predominates: blood (sanguine, warm-hearted and volatile), black bile (melancholic and sad), yellow bile (choleric and quick to anger and action) and phlegm (phlegmatic, sluggish and apathetic).

Hahnemann also suggested the existence of a few primary causes of acute and chronic illnesses, which he believed corresponded with Galen's body types and which he called *miasms*. The first miasm, known as *psora* (itch), refers to a general susceptibility to disease and was considered by Hahnemann to be the source of all chronic disease. His other two miasms were the sexually transmitted diseases syphilis and sycosis (gonorrhea). He considered these three conditions to be the cause of at least 80 percent of all diseases.

To be fair, homeopathy has made several important yet indirect contributions to the practice of medicine. First, it helped rid the medical profession of awful practices such as bleeding. Second, it was the initial inspiration for useful drugs such as nitroglycerin and aconite. Third, it has been credited with providing early support for some important components of scientific medicine, including clinical trials with control groups, systematic and quantitative procedures, and the use of statistics.

For several reasons, it is curious that homeopathy is even proposed as a therapy for horses. Hahnemann did none of his work on animals. Psora, syphilis, and gonorrhea are not conditions recognized in animals. Prescribing medications for animals based on how they make people feel would seem a misguided approach, and the concept of tailoring prescriptions to body types and personalities also wouldn't seem to apply to horses.

THE PHYSICS OF HOMEOPATHY

If homeopathic remedies are effective, then how do they work? No one knows. If they do work, they must do so in a way that violates established principles of physics, chemistry and pharmacology or in a way that is yet to be discovered. As one early critic of homeopathy wrote, "Either Hahnemann is right, in which case our science and the basis of our thinking is nonsense, or he is wrong, in which case this teaching is nonsense."[3]

Homeopathic remedies are diluted by a factor of either 10 or 100. D dilutions are prepared by serial dilutions of 1:9; C dilutions are prepared by serial dilutions of 1:100. A remedy marked

C30 implies a 1:99 dilution performed thirty times. Using simple mathematics, it can be calculated that at dilutions of C12 or D24 or greater, the remedies are unlikely to contain even a single molecule of the original substance.

THE MILLION-DOLLAR DUCK

Every year Boiron, a French manufacturer of homeopathic remedies, selects a duck and removes its liver and heart. After the organs are ground up and marinated, the extracts are diluted in homeopathic fashion and become the basis for a flu remedy called Oscillococcinum, which is sold worldwide.

The dilution, according to the remedy's container, is 200C, which is a dilution of 1:99 repeated 200 times. What this means is that the odds are 1 in 10^{400} that even one molecule of the duck will end up in a pill. It's an amazingly economical strategy for Boiron, because a single duck can easily supply all the world's needs for the product. (Perhaps that's why it's been called the "million-dollar duck.")

Given that the original substance is not present in extremely dilute homeopathic remedies, people who seek to explain how homeopathy might work have had to come up with some pretty fanciful explanations, such as the formation of stable ice crystals, magnetic properties of water or the formation of protein shells in the water mixture. The problem with these concepts is that they don't agree with anything that is known to exist. For example, it's unlikely that water could maintain a complex ice-like structure under all that shaking, and water isn't magnetic. And so it goes.

When structural changes in matter do occur, they are fairly easy to demonstrate, using such techniques as transmission electron microscopy, spectroscopy, ultraviolet transmission characteristics, radiographs and ultrasound. If structural changes in the composition of homeopathic remedies exist, then they should be relatively easy to detect. But such changes have not been demonstrated.

One could hypothesize that there exists some sort of biologic effect of homeopathic medications that is independent of known physical laws. Of course, this sort of speculation would be practically impossible to test. It is known, though, that no known substance fits such a description, and appealing to unknown laws to explain undocumented phenomena falls outside the framework of legitimate science.

Further physical difficulties with the concept of homeopathic dilutions relate to the fact that many such remedies come in the form of lactose tablets. The homeopathic dilution is applied to the pill, which serves as a carrier. The diluted liquid naturally evaporates, which begs the question of how the homeopathic substance is transferred from liquid to tablet. Other questions include why the diluted mixture would "remember" only the healing powers of the active substance but would "forget" the side effects or why the water doesn't "remember" other things with which it has been in contact.

TEST-TUBE STUDIES

In 1988, the mainstream science journal *Nature* jumped to the forefront of the controversy by publishing the first paper to support homeopathy's claims. The writers suggested that extremely dilute solutions of a human antiserum caused changes in certain blood cells known as basophils. Even though the experimental model chosen is known to be extremely unstable, *Nature* couldn't find any flaws in the study, so out it came. After the issue was published, however, *Nature* sent a team of investigators to the writers' laboratory; the team concluded that the original investigation contained serious flaws. A war of words ensued, but the gist of the matter is that in at least three separate investigations that used identical or similar experimental models, researchers failed to reproduce the initial study's results.

REVIEWS AND META-ANALYSES

Several reviews and meta-analyses of homeopathy have been performed. The list of reviews in this chapter is not complete, but no review or meta-analysis exists to show that homeopathy is effective. Nevertheless, the results are open to some interpretation: You can find reviews that use the same studies to support wildly different conclusions. To avoid confusion, the conclusions of some of the studies will be quoted instead of citing individual bits of data out of context.

I. A 1985 chapter on veterinary homeopathy came to this conclusion:

Contrary to what you hear or read too often, rigorous scientific demonstration of the therapeutic effect of homeopathic remedies in veterinary medicine has not yet been done. Although it may seem exaggerated to conclude that homeopathy has absolutely no place, from a pragmatic point of view (and relative among animal owners . . .), in veterinary medicine, it is obvious that future works will have to bend to the new modern methodologies in order to be able to take away the firm beliefs of stern minds.[4]

2. A 1990 review of forty published randomized trials of medical homeopathy found that most of the studies had major methodological flaws and concluded that "The results do not provide acceptable evidence that homeopathic treatments are effective."[5]

3. A 1991 meta-analysis of medical homeopathy concluded, "At the moment the evidence of clinical trials is positive but not sufficient to draw definitive conclusions because most trials are of low methodological quality and because of the unknown role of publication bias." The investigators also noted that, "Critical people who do not believe in the efficacy of homeopathy before reading the evidence presented here probably will still not be convinced; people who were more ambivalent in advance will perhaps have a more optimistic view now, whereas people who already believed in the efficacy of homeopathy might at this moment be almost certain that homeopathy works."[6]

4. A 1992 German review concluded that "Due to the advance of alternative medicine, a critical synopsis by means of the comparison between scientific medicine (clinical medicine) and homeopathy is warranted. The review of studies carried out according to current scientific criteria revealed—at best—a placebo effect of homeopathy. Until now there is no proven mechanism for the mode of action of homeopathy."[7]

5. A 1993 German review of homeopathy in veterinary medicine draws several conclusions:

- "Doctor and veterinarian are similarly obligated to apply the therapeutic measure that prevailing opinions deem most effective. Where there is for particular definite illnesses a particularly effective and generally recognized treatment, in such cases the supporters of homeopathy may not disregard the better successes from their own differing direction."

- "It is undisputed that homeopathy in the area of stronger potency can achieve effects pharmacologically and toxicologically; the superiority of homeopathy as a therapeutic measure in comparison with conventional therapy methods is at this point not verified. Moreover, the harmlessness of homeopathy in stronger potency is for the most part not verified."

- "The effectiveness of homeopathy in middle and high potencies is up to now not verified. It is undisputed that with the help of homeopathy, not insignificant placebo effects can be achieved. In veterinary medicine, giving an animal an 'active' placebo and another a 'passive' one can play a significant role and influence the owner."[8]

6. A 1994 review and meta-analysis of serial agitated dilutions (SADs) in experimental toxicology stated, "As with clinical studies, the overall quality of toxicology research using SAD preparations is low. The majority of studies either could not be reevaluated by the reviewers or were of such low quality that their likelihood of validity is doubtful. The number of methodologically sound, independently reproduced studies is too small to make any definitive conclusions regarding the effect of SAD preparations in toxicology."[9]

7. A 1997 meta-analysis concluded, "The results of our meta-analysis are not compatible with the hypothesis that the clinical effects of homeopathy are completely due to placebo. However, we found insufficient evidence from these studies that homeopathy is clearly effective for any single clinical condition."[10]

8. A 1998 review of homeopathic treatment in animals suggested approaching the therapy with an "open mind." As evidence for the treatment's effectiveness, the study cited thirteen studies that found some clinical evidence of effectiveness, seven whose results were difficult to interpret for various reasons, and six that found no response to treatment or a worsening of the condition. Several of the studies cited were performed on healthy animals. In one study, in which sick animals got sicker after treatment, the worsening of their health was taken as possible evidence of the treatment's effectiveness, according to "Herring's Law."[11] Of course, such a law would mean that you can't lose when administering homeopathic medications, because whether the patient improves or worsens, you can view the treatment as successful.

Properly blinded, randomized experiments with high-dilution homeopathic preparations and both a placebo group and a known-effective-treatment group with a large number of animals and predefined outcome variables that examine the effect on diseases are absent in veterinary homeopathy. To date, no single study of homeopathy showing positive results in animals has been replicated successfully.

The lack of good evidence of effectiveness of homeopathic remedies may not matter to supporters of homeopathy. One leading advocate of homeopathy has asserted that it is not important to prove the therapy's effectiveness through scientific research and suggests that personal experience is more important that any number of carefully controlled studies. (Of course, if you believe that something is going to work, it just might.)

IS HOMEOPATHY SAFE?

Most researchers believe that homeopathic remedies are largely safe—not an unexpected finding, given that most homeopathic solutions appear to contain none of the original substance. Adverse reactions in humans to homeopathic medications have been reported infrequently, with symptoms ranging from severe itching and a measles-like skin rash to anaphylactic shock and inflammation of the pancreas. One can conclude, then, that although high-dilution remedies may be safe, remedies that contain the original substance may not be.

Another safety concern related to homeopathy stems from some practitioners' advising their clients against obtaining routine immunizations. This advice has even been published in equine health magazines. The origin of homeopathic antipathy to vaccination is unknown; Hahnemann's writings contain no condemnations of immunization.

AND YOU THOUGHT FAST FOOD WAS SUSPECT . . .

Think some common drugs have weird origins? To name a couple, penicillin comes from mold, and estrogen-replacement therapy comes from the urine of pregnant mares. But these are tame compared to some of the origins of homeopathic remedies.

Homeopathic remedies have fancy Latin names—perhaps to hide the common names. *Castor Equi* (thumbnail of horse) is recommended for cracked or sore nipples, and *Lac caninum* (dog's milk) is used to treat human mastitis. *Lachesis* (venom of the South American bushmaster snake) is for menopausal symptoms. *Natrum mur* (common table salt) supposedly helps cold sores. *Apis mellifica* (crushed honeybee) is for acute arthritis. Perhaps the variety of these and other remedies is proof of an undiluted sense of humor among Hahnemann's followers.

A final concern is some homeopathic practitioners' use of homeopathic vaccines or *nosodes* prepared from high dilutions of infectious agents—material such as vomitus, discharges, fecal matter and infected tissue. Hahnemann himself was against the use of such preparations, and there is absolutely no evidence to suggest that such "immunizations" have any benefit. In one case reported in the medical literature, a patient followed her homeopath's advice and received a homeopathic immunization against malaria before a trip to an endemic area. She promptly contracted malaria. Homeopathic nosodes have also failed to keep dogs from dying of parvoviral enteritis.

IMPLICATIONS FOR THE HORSE OWNER

As one report notes, "There are as many homeopathies as there are homeopaths." The ready availability of mass-marketed, over-the-counter homeopathic remedies appears to violate Hahnemann's principle of tailoring the therapy to the patient's symptoms. Homeopathy's philosophy of basing treatment on symptoms would seem to contradict claims that it addresses the needs of the "whole patient." Add these contradictions to the fact that nothing in the history of homeopathy suggests that it's an effective treatment for horses, and you've got quite a puzzling mix.

More than 200 years after Hahnemann's work, homeopathy has never been proven to be effective in treating a single condition. So why do some people insist that it works? One simple explanation would be that it is a placebo. If homeopathic medications are placebos, naturally you wouldn't be able to identify the physical mechanism by which they work. Clinical trials would be comparing one placebo to another, which naturally would produce confusing, disappointing and/or irreproducible results. As for safety, higher-dilution medications would pose no threat because they'd merely be water, water/alcohol mixtures or lactose tablets.

Homeopathic remedies do not appear to be effective treatments for any condition in human or veterinary medicine, nor is there evidence that they are superior to established therapies. It is *possible* that some future study will show homeopathic medications to be effective, but the preponderance of evidence to date is that they are not.

MAHLON WAGNER

Mahlon Wagner, Ph.D., is professor emeritus of psychology at the State University of New York-Oswego. He holds a B.S. in chemistry from Bucknell University and a Ph.D. in psychology from the University of Rochester. In 1989, he received a Fulbright research scholarship to do a cross-cultural examination of skeptical beliefs on alternative medicine and the paranormal at Justus-Liebig University in Giessen, Germany.

NOTES

1. Hahnemann, S. *Organon of Medicine*, 6th ed. Calcutta: M. Bhattacharyya, 1960. Pages 7–288.

2. Hahnemann, S. *The Chronic Diseases.* New York: n.p., 1846. Page 141.

3. Jürgenson, T. "The Scientific Art of Healing and Its Opponents" (in German). *Volkmanns Sammlung Klinisher Vorträge* 106(1876): 876–916.

4. Aulas, J. J. *Veterinary Homeopathy: Historic Approach and Scientific Critique and Evaluation of Its Empiric Foundation and Therapeutic Efficacy* (in French). Paris: Roland Bettex, 1985. Pages 209–224.

5. Hill, C., and Doyon, F. R. "Review of Randomized Trials of Homeopathy." *Rev. Epidem. et Santé Publ.* 38(1990): 139–147.

6. Kleijnen, J., Knipschild, P., and Ter Riet, G. "Clinical Trials of Homeopathy." *BMJ* 302(1991): 316–323.

7. Kurz, R. "Clinical Medicine Versus Homeopathy" (in German). *Padiatr. Padol.* 27(1992): 37–41.

8. Löscher, W. "Homeopathy in Veterinary Medicine: Critical Thoughts from the View of Pharmacology" (in German). *Unconventional Medical Procedures* (in German). Stuttgart: Gustav Fischer Verlag, 1993. Pages 273–302.

9. Linde, K., et al. "Critical Review and Meta-Analysis of Serial Agitated Dilutions in Experimental Toxicology." *Hm. Exper. Toxicol.* 13(1994): 481–492.

10. Linde, K., et al. "Are the Clinical Effects of Homeopathy Placebo Effects? A Meta-Analysis of Placebo-Controlled Trials." *Lancet* 350(1997): 834–843.

11. Wynn, S. G. "Studies on Use of Homeopathy in Animals." *JAVMA* 212(5) (1998): 719–724.

CHAPTER THIRTEEN

Herbal Therapy

with Joy Reighard, Ph.D.

If you're looking for a more "natural" way to help your sick or injured horse, you'll probably check out one or more of the many herbal products. After all, what could be better for your horse than nature's own botanicals?

From ancient Chinese practices to the Thomsonian movement of the late 1700s, using herbs to aid healing is a long-standing tradition—a fact that reassures many of today's users of herbs' safety and trustworthiness. However, many issues involved with herbal medications must be addressed before you can be assured that they are safe and effective therapies for horses.

HERBS ARE DRUGS!

Many of today's medicines were derived from plants. Digitalis, which is used in the treatment of congestive heart failure, originally was derived from dried leaves of the foxglove plant (*Digitalis purpurea*). In 200 B.C., the Greek physician Hippocrates prescribed the bark and leaves of the willow tree (rich in a substance first called salicin) to relieve pain and fever. Some 2,000 years later, a German chemist created salicyclic acid (aspirin) by isolating and chemically stabilizing salicin. In short, when herbs are effective medications, it is for one simple reason: Effective herbal products contain active pharmacological ingredients—they're not benign, harmless substances.

The statement that some medicines are derived from plants also is misleading, however. Herbs may contain any number of substances with biological activity. For example, the foxglove plant contains more than thirty glycosides, all of which can affect the heart in different ways. And although willow bark may have some anti-inflammatory effect when chewed, it also contains large amounts of tannins, which can be very upsetting to the stomach.

Because of the limited number of studies done on herbs, it's impossible for today's consumer to know about an herbal remedy's every component and its pharmacological and possible toxic effects. According to one study, approximately 7,000 species of plants are used in China as herbal remedies, but only 230 of the most commonly used plants have been subjected to in-depth pharmacological, analytical and clinical studies.

Further complicating the problem is the fact that the active-ingredient content of herbs in their natural state can vary greatly from plant to plant. For example, glycyrrhizic acid, one of the main pharmacological agents in licorice root, occurs naturally in concentrations ranging on the average from 2 to 7 percent, with some plants as high as 27 percent in rare cases. In large amounts, glycyrrhizic acid can be toxic. The fact that different plants have varying concentrations of the active ingredient makes accurate dosing impossible.

The fact that some herbs have active pharmacological ingredients can be a problem for unsuspecting horse owners and trainers.

Numerous horses have tested positive for substances forbidden by the sport associations under which they compete after having been administered one or more commercially available herbal products. For example:

1. Spinach octacosanol tablets were shown to be contaminated with phenylpropanolamine, a stimulant, after a horse racing at Santa Anita in California tested positive for the substance.

2. Numerous trainers in the United States have been penalized when their horses tested positive for caffeine after receiving various herbal products containing guarana. Guarana, made from the crushed seed of a climbing shrub native to Brazil and Uruguay, is used to prepare a beverage in those countries. Some of these products are labeled "no added caffeine" although guarana, which contains caffeine, is the obvious source.

3. Some herbal products containing ginseng can produce a positive drug test for caffeine.

4. Various herbal products contain plant parts of ephedra, which contains ephedrine, a drug that produces dramatic effects on the cardiovascular system. Some of these products, such as "herbal ecstasy," also contain caffeine. Racehorses taking these products have tested positive for ephedrine, phenypropanolamine, pseudoephedrine, norpseudoephedrine and caffeine.

THE MYTH OF "NATURAL"

Many manufacturers of "natural" herbal products claim that their products are somehow superior to laboratory-synthesized products that contain the same active ingredients. There is no scientific basis for such claims: A chemical is a chemical. For example, there is no difference in the vitamin C obtained from natural biosynthetic processes in rose hips and that which is made in a chemical manufacturer's laboratory. Your horse's "drug receptors" cannot distinguish whether a molecule comes from a chemical laboratory or from the plant kingdom. The word *natural* implies only the source of the product, not that the product is of higher quality or better for you or your horse—although "natural" products usually come with a bigger price tag.

"Natural" does not mean that an herbal medication is safe or harmless, either. Naturally occurring toxins are just as hazardous as synthetic toxins. For instance, cabbage and broccoli contain a chemical whose breakdown products act the same as dioxin, one of the most feared industrial contaminants. One reason herbal products may be thought of as less toxic is that they tend to contain very small amounts of the active ingredients. Toxic effects are dose-related, so it stands to reason that herbal products may be less toxic than products that contain larger amounts of the ingredients in question.

HERBAL REMEDIES AND HEALTH RISKS

Herbs may be "natural" but that does not also mean that they are risk free. There are good reasons why you might think twice before feeding your horse herbs.

DIRECT RISKS

Most horse owners know that some plants, such as *Senecio* sp. a selenium-accumulator, are toxic to horses. Unfortunately, no good studies have been performed on the effects of herbal products on horses. However, numerous documented examples of direct health risks from natural plants and herbs exist in the medical field.

For example, various studies show that certain naturally occurring chemicals in food can cause cancer in humans. The phorbol esters present in the Euphorbiacea family, some of which are used as folk remedies or herb teas, can cause cell abnormalities and are thought to be a cause of nasopharyngeal cancer in China and esophageal cancer in Curacao. They also have been shown to cause signs of general poisoning in lactating goats and their milk-fed kids.

Pyrrolizidine toxins found in comfrey tea, various herbal medicines and some foods can cause liver cancer in rats, cirrhosis of the liver and other diseases. Tea-tree oil, a common ingredient in some "natural" fly repellents for horses, is known to cause skin irritation in people and has been reported to do the same in horses. Allergic reactions, toxic reactions and possible effects on dividing cells have been reported in humans who used various herbal preparations.

HERBS: MEDICINE OR FOOD?

The Dietary Supplement Health and Education Act of 1994 included herbal products in its definition of dietary supplements, even though herbs have little or no nutritional value. Herbal or other botanical ingredients include processed or unprocessed plant parts (bark, leaves, flowers, fruits and stems) as well as extracts and essential oils. They are available as teas, powders, tablets, capsules and elixirs and may be marketed as single substances or combined with other herbs, vitamins, minerals, amino acids or non-nutrient ingredients. The bill, which seriously weakened the Food and Drug Administration's (FDA) regulation of herbs and dietary supplements, was spearheaded by the health-food industry.

Even if an herb is known to be toxic, it may not necessarily be removed from the marketplace; the FDA usually issues a warning rather than a ban in such cases. Its Center for Food Safety and Applied Nutrition maintains a searchable database (http://vm.cfsan.fda.gov/) of reports received of adverse reactions associated with the use of dietary supplements and herbal products.[1]

INDIRECT RISKS

Even when herbal preparations don't pose a direct health risk, using them may present indirect risks if doing so delays or replaces an effective form of conventional treatment, which can happen if the provider is overly optimistic about his or her abilities or if a user puts too much faith in the healing powers of nature.

Horses, too, may be subjected to indirect health risks from the use of herbal remedies. An example would be an herbalist's advocating the use of a natural remedy (such as garlic) to prevent and treat internal parasites. Considering that no natural remedy has been shown to be effective in controlling internal parasites, dosing your horse with garlic for that purpose is certainly not in its best health interests.

The use of herbal medicines also means that there is a potential for drug interactions between these preparations and conventional medicines. A number of interactions of this type have been reported in human medicine. These include reactions between papaya extract and warfarin (an agent that prevents blood clotting) and evening primrose oil and drugs that potentially cause seizures. However, different compounds can interact in unexpected ways. More studies on interactions between traditional and modern medicines are certainly needed.

LACK OF QUALITY ASSURANCE

Herbs for horses are marketed as foods or dietary supplements and therefore are not regulated in the same manner as drugs are. Herbal-remedy manufacturers do not have to meet federal standards for processing, harvesting, packaging, quality or purity. Most herbal-product labels lack information about side effects, dangers, contraindications, dosages and even contents and potency. Because these products aren't regulated, it's virtually impossible to know what your horse is getting when you give it an herbal supplement. Some manufacturers are beginning to "standardize" their products on their own by indicating the amount of one ingredient, presumably the most active compound, per dose on the label and advertising the product as "standardized." However, even if you could obtain accurate information about the contents of a product and determine its proper dosage and route of administration, you wouldn't have solved the problem of shared common names.

Very few herbal-remedy labels list the herb's scientific name along with its common name; the problem is that several herbs may share the same common name. Six very different plants, for example, go by the common name of snakeroot. The various sub-species of ginseng each have different properties and costs. If you don't know exactly what you're getting, you may be buying a less-effective or even completely nonmedicinal herb. In fact, according to some authorities the more expensive the plant material, the more likely it is to be of inferior quality.

Just because a product contains herbs doesn't mean that those herbs do anything either. Herbs such as burdock root, cleavers (derived from a climbing plant that is common in England), oregano and dandelion have no known therapeutic value, but all are listed as ingredients in an over-the-counter herbal anti-itch preparation sold to horse owners.

ADULTERATED PRODUCTS

Reports exist of herbal medications that were adulterated with phar-maceuticals, contaminants or erroneous substitutes for the primary herbal ingredient. Adulteration of herbal products appears to be particularly problematic in (but not limited to) Chinese herbal medications. People have been severely or even fatally poisoned after taking herbal remedies containing aconitine, podophyllin, heavy metals and other toxic substances.

A recent study of Chinese herbal medications found that an average of 23.7 percent were adulterated with everything from nonsteroidal anti-inflammatory drugs to caffeine; more than half of the adulterated products contained two or more adulterants. Similarly, eight of eleven Chinese dermatologic creams had high concentrations of corticosteroids. In Belgium, at least 100 cases of a fatal kidney problem occurred in women who had followed a weight-loss regimen that included the use of Chinese herbs. The culprit was an herb that had inadvertently been used as a substitute for the prescribed Chinese herb.

THE LIMITATIONS OF TRADITION

Over the years, folk healers and traditional herbalists have accumulated quite a bit of information about herbs and their effects. Their experience may be of value, but folklore is not of much help in detecting adverse effects, such as cancer, that may occur years after a patient takes an herbal remedy or that occur only in a small percentage of cases.

To illustrate the limitations of traditional experience, statisticians can point to the "rule of three," which states that the number of patients treated must be three times greater than the frequency of bad reactions to have a 95-percent chance that the therapist will witness the reaction. In other words, if an adverse reaction occurs in every 1,000 cases, the therapist would have to treat at least 3,000 patients to be 95-percent sure that he or she will see one reaction. To have a 95-percent chance of seeing a 1-in-1,000 reaction three times, the therapist would have to treat 6,500 patients with the same remedy, or approximately one patient a day for twenty-five years.

THE ROLE OF PHARMACEUTICALS

When researchers identify substances of pharmaceutical value in plants, drug companies try to isolate and reproduce that substance in order to provide a reliable supply. They also attempt to make synthetic versions that are more potent and predictable and that have fewer side effects. Pharmaceutical products derived from herbs are likely to be more active and more selective and to have fewer side effects than the "natural" products. If herbal products were as effective as the derivatives patented by the pharmaceutical companies, the pharmaceutical industry wouldn't exist; companies would just sell herbal products.

IMPLICATIONS FOR THE HORSE OWNER

Although there is a growing body of scientific literature on herbal remedies, studies to determine whether particular compounds cause birth defects or cancer are exceedingly rare. It is practically impossible to find research that compares the effects of differing herb dosages so that you can determine the appropriate level of treatment. Plus, very little is known about whether herbs even enter the bloodstream or if they do, how long they remain.

COMMON "HORSE HERBS": AN EXPERT'S ASSESSMENT

If you open an equine herbal remedy catalog, chances are you'll see the following herbs. Here's what independent herbal remedy expert Dr. Varro Tyler had to say about them in his book *The Honest Herbal* (New York: Pharmaceutical Products Press, 1993):

* *Burdock:* "In spite of its long use as a folkloric remedy, no solid evidence exists that burdock exhibits any useful therapeutic activity."

- *Comfrey:* "Although comfrey is presently one of the most common herbs sold to the American public, there is reason to believe that using it internally is definitely hazardous to the health."

- *Dandelion:* "No significant therapeutic benefits should be expected from the use of any dandelion product."

- *Fenugreek:* "Fenugreek is soothing, flavorful and even nutritious. Although it is not a potent medicament, it is quite harmless in normal use."

- *Red clover:* "None of these various pigments, phenolic compounds, tannins and the like [in red clover] has any pronounced therapeutic value."

- *Yucca:* "No proper scientific evidence exists that yucca tablets are helpful in treating rheumatoid or osteoarthritis."

No studies or reports on herbal remedies' interactions with drugs, foods or other herbs in horses have been conducted. A veterinarian who wants to prescribe herbal remedies can study only the herb's main mechanism of action, make assumptions about the content of the product, try to spot potentially hazardous interactions and hope for the best. If you're a layperson who wants to treat your horse yourself, you have even less knowledge about herbs and pharmacology than your vet does.

If you're determined to give your horse an herbal product, make sure the one you choose is standardized. Limit your use of herbs to the treatment of less-serious, self-limiting ailments; don't rely on herbal therapies if your horse's condition is potentially serious. Dr. Tyler warns that consumers are "less likely to receive value for money spent in the field of herbal medicine than in almost any other." With safe and effective pharmaceutical products available, treatment with herbs rarely makes sense.

JOY REIGHARD

Joy Reighard, Ph.D., received her B.S. in pharmacy and her Ph.D. in *pharmacognosy* (the science of determining pharmacologically active substances in plants) from the University of Pittsburgh School of Pharmacy. She is a licensed pharmacist in Pennsylvania. An associate professor of pharmacognosy at Philadelphia's Temple University School of Pharmacy, she has taught an elective course in veterinary pharmacy since 1988. She edits the newsletters of the American Society of Pharmacognosy and the Temple University School of Pharmacy.

NOTES

1. Barrett, S., M.D. "The Herbal Minefield." From the Web site www.quackwatch. com/01QuackeryRelatedTopics/herbs.html, January 1999. Used with permission.

CHAPTER FOURTEEN

Nutraceuticals

with Kathleen Crandell, Ph.D. and Stephen Duren, Ph.D.

Since the early 1990s, the horse world has witnessed the explosive growth of a multimillion-dollar industry: the nutraceutical industry. The term *nutraceutical*, a hybrid of *nutrient* (a food) and *pharmaceutical* (a drug), is used to describe a wide variety of products that are marketed as dietary supplements but that supposedly work to treat or prevent disease. The concept of nutraceuticals raises many questions: How are they classified legally? How do they differ from nutrients and drugs? What rules govern their safety and efficacy? What nutraceuticals have found their way into the horse industry? And, of course, do they work?

DEFINITIONS

For starters, several terms need to be explained:

I. *Nutrient:* As defined in 1996 by the Association of American Feed Control Officials (AAFCO), a nutrient is "a feed constituent in a form and at a level that will help support the life of an animal." The primary nutrients are proteins, fats, carbohydrates, minerals and vitamins.

2. *Feed:* As defined in 1996 by AAFCO, feed is "edible materials which are consumed by animals and contribute energy and/or nutrients to the animal's diet." Given this definition, you can classify just about anything a horse eats as feed.

3. *Food:* As defined in 1968 by the Food, Drug and Cosmetic Act, a food is "an article that provides taste, aroma or nutritive value. The Food and Drug Administration (FDA) considers food as 'generally recognized as safe' (GRAS)."

4. *Drug:* As defined in 1996 by AAFCO, a drug is "a substance intended for use in the diagnosis, cure, mitigation, treatment or prevention of disease in man or other animals. A substance other than food intended to affect the structure or any function of the body of man or other animals."

5. *Dietary supplement:* As defined in 1994 by the Dietary Supplement Health and Education Act (DSHEA), it is "a product that contains one or more of the following dietary ingredients: vitamin, mineral, herb or other botanical, and amino acid (protein). Includes any possible component of the diet as well as concentrates, constituents, extracts or metabolites of these compounds."

6. *Nutraceutical:* No generally accepted definition exists, but the dietary supplement industry appears to use the term to refer to any nontoxic food component that may also have health benefits, including disease treatment and prevention.

7. *Veterinary nutraceutical:* As defined by the newly created North American Veterinarian Nutraceutical Council, Inc. (NAVNC), "a substance which is produced in a purified or extracted form and administered orally to patients to provide agents required for normal body structure and function and administered with the intent of improving the health and well-being of animals." (Note the absence of any reference to science or proof.)

FOOD OR DRUG?

One potential difference between a feed and a nutraceutical is that whereas a feed is required to have nutritive value and is accountable (via labeling) for these values, a nutraceutical is unlikely to have established nutritive value. Another difference is that feed is generally recognized as safe (GRAS). Although nutraceuticals may contain natural substances, they may not be GRAS.

The other big difference between a food and a nutraceutical, of course, involves the concepts of disease treatment and prevention and the improvement of animals' health and well-being. When a dietary supplement is intended to be used to treat or prevent disease, it falls under the classification of a drug by default. Drugs must be proven safe and effective in a rigorous approval process before they can be marketed to the public, and a manufacturer's failure to secure the necessary approvals may result in regulatory action. But makers of nutraceuticals don't have to get their products approved, so their products technically can't be considered drugs.

It appears that the nutraceuticals industry is trying to stake out some middle ground between food and drug—a position with several unique advantages. If nutraceuticals aren't foods, the manufacturers don't have to label their products with nutrient profiles, the way feed manufacturers do. If nutraceuticals aren't drugs, the manufacturers don't have to get their products tested or approved, but they can claim that the products aid in the treatment or prevention of disease (within limits, anyway).

Take vitamin E as an example. Added to the diet as an essential nutrient, it is considered a feed component. Claimed to treat or prevent azoturia (tying-up) in horses, it is considered a drug. So which is it? From a manufacturer's standpoint, the ideal is for a product not to be classified as a drug but still to be perceived as therapeutic.

REGULATORY ISSUES

The primary set of rules governing the human-nutraceutical market is the 1994 Dietary Supplement Health and Education Act (DSHEA), which does not permit the FDA to consider a new product a drug or a food additive if it falls under the definition of a dietary supplement. A dietary supplement can be just about any possible dietary component or a concentrate, constituent, extract or metabolite of a component. DSHEA shifts the burden of proving a substance's safety from the manufacturer to the FDA, which must prove that a substance is unsafe.

Horse owners, take note: DSHEA rules do not apply to nutraceuticals intended for animals, because the federal government claims that metabolic differences between humans and animals and potential safety issues concerning nutraceuticals administered to animals used for food, (such as residues in tissues), are reasons to exclude animals from provisions of the DSHEA. The point is that, at present, these products really aren't regulated.

AAFCO's board of directors recently formed the Nutraceutical Regulatory Advisory Panel, which is charged with drafting a national consensus on a regulatory approach to nutraceutical use.

The panel sent out a questionnaire to consumers, health professionals and industry representatives to learn about the issues in question. The advisory panel recommended that products calling themselves nutraceuticals should be regulated. They also suggested evaluating each nutraceutical on a case-by-case basis to classify it as a food, a food additive or a drug. For instance, if a manufacturer claims that its product treats, prevents, cures or mitigates a disease or affects the body's structure or function in a manner unrelated to nutrition, the product would be considered a drug and would fall under the FDA's jurisdiction.

ARE NUTRACEUTICALS SAFE? DO THEY WORK?

First and foremost, nutraceuticals should be safe. But like many substances, they have the potential to cause harm. They can be toxic, or their use can delay effective treatment for a serious condition.

There is good news and bad news in the area of nutraceutical safety. The good news is that it's relatively easy to establish the safety of such products through studies in which subjects receive greater-than-recommended test doses and any adverse reactions are noted. The bad news is that such studies generally have not been conducted. Thus, a lack of reported toxicity problems with a nutraceutical is not evidence of its safety.

Are nutraceuticals effective? Hard to say. You can evaluate a conventional drug's effectiveness by looking at studies that document the structure of the compound, how quickly it's removed from the horse's body, where in the body it travels and other important characteristics. The data on a drug can be classified as *pharmaceutical* (evaluations of manufacturing quality, purity and labeling accuracy), *pharmacokinetic* (the drug's path though the animal's body and its absorption, tissue distribution, metabolism and excretion), and *pharmacodynamic* (the animal's response to the drug). It's most difficult to establish pharmacodynamic data for nutraceuticals, because most of them produce a cascade of reactions throughout the body.

THE CHANGING CONVENTIONAL WISDOM

Beta carotene is a vitamin A precursor that's found in dark green and yellow vegetables and fruits (and carrots). Following test-tube and animal studies as well as small-scale medical studies, it was widely promoted as a cancer preventive or cure. However, several large epidemiological studies found that it either had no effect on cancer rates or slightly increased smokers' chances of developing lung cancer. This is one of the best examples of why you shouldn't necessarily follow the current nutritional wisdom blindly—especially if it's being disseminated by supplement manufacturers.

In the booming, poorly regulated nutraceuticals market, many products have not been tested for either safety or efficacy. A good number of them appear to make unsupported drug claims without proper data to support their safety and efficacy. Before you buy, ask to see peer-reviewed and published research data that support the product's claims.

NUTRACEUTICALS AND YOUR HORSE

The general theory behind nutraceuticals is that they increase or replace the supply of natural building blocks in your horse's body to diminish the signs of disease (such as degenerative joint disease) or to improve performance. This theory has a flaw that's obvious to biochemists: The body's reactions generally are not limited by the amount of raw materials available and supplying more of those materials isn't necessarily helpful.

Of course, substance deficiencies (such as in vitamins or minerals) can exist and can impair the body's functioning; a vitamin E deficiency has been implicated in a condition called equine motor neuron disease, for example. But nutraceutical manufacturers aren't marketing their products as treatments for deficiencies; they're implying that with a larger amount of certain raw materials, your horse's body can perform more efficiently—the "more is better" approach. In truth, the body (both the horse's and yours) does one of three things when it's given an excess of any substance: it stores it (the way extra calories are stored as fat), it eliminates it (the most common occurrence) or it develops a toxic reaction to the excess.

As is the case with most of the other therapies discussed in this book, the lion's share of the research on nutraceuticals has been conducted on humans, not on animals. The nutraceutical ingredients listed in the following sections have had at least preliminary testing in the horse. The section explains each substance's theorized mode of action, and summarizes the results of studies in both humans and horses.

CARNITINE

Carnitine is an amino acid found in large amounts in heart and skeletal muscle. Your horse's muscle cells need carnitine to help them convert fatty acids to energy. Some researchers have hypothesized that extra dietary carnitine encourages the muscle cells to use fats rather than stored carbohydrates (known as *glycogen*) in the production of energy. Glycogen use produces a by-product called lactic acid, and lactic acid is associated with muscle fatigue. The theory is that carnitine supplementation reduces the body's dependence on glycogen, thereby resulting in decreased lactic-acid production and improved muscle functioning and endurance.

Studies in healthy humans have not shown that carnitine supplementation increases the amount of carnitine in the muscles or results in improved athletic performance. The healthy human body appears to produce adequate carnitine (primarily in the liver) under normal conditions, but stress and certain diseases could potentially lead to deficiencies.

Most people who eat meat consume plenty of dietary carnitine; but horses, who are herbivores, do not. Horses' bodies have to generate the majority of their carnitine supply. Researchers have studied the effects of dietary carnitine supplementation in yearlings and adult horses, but the results are somewhat inconclusive. In the short term, the extra carnitine did increase the amount of the substance in the blood; but long-term supplementation did not appear to increase the amount of carnitine in the muscle. Because an increase in muscle carnitine presumably would be the determining factor in improving performance, it can safely be said that, to date, no evidence exists that carnitine supplementation benefits equine athletic performance.

COENZYME Q_{10}

Ubiquinone (more commonly known as Coenzyme Q_{10}) occurs naturally in the horse's body. It is used in the chemical pathways that produce energy, and it works in concert with other substances to regenerate cellular energy. Coenzyme Q_{10} also functions as a powerful antioxidant and free-radical scavenger. (An *antioxidant* is a substance that gives up electrons easily; as such, it may be able to enter into chemical reactions that act to neutralize harmful inflammatory compounds, such as oxidants and free radicals.)

People who suffer from cardiovascular or periodontal disease have been shown to have lower-than-normal levels of coenzyme Q_{10}; what's not clear is whether the low levels caused the problems or whether the problems caused the low levels. In any case, coenzyme Q_{10} supplementation is reported to have helped in the treatment of heart problems, muscular dystrophy, muscle problems and periodontal disease.

The effects of coenzyme Q_{10} in the horse are not well-researched. One study found that it might indirectly affect the rate that bodily tissues use oxygen, but dietary supplementation did not affect important indicators of exercise efficiency such as lactic acid metabolism or heart rate. Coenzyme Q_{10} has potential in treating equine heart and muscle disorders, but further research is needed.

CREATINE

Creatine phosphate (PCr) is a substance that's normally present in limited amounts in muscle cells. A simple reaction involving PCr is the muscle cell's first and fastest source of energy. Some researchers have proposed that inadequate PCr is one of the most likely causes of poor performance during intense, fatiguing, short-duration exercise. They hope that increasing muscles' creatine content through dietary supplementation will lead to a corresponding increase in PCr concentration.

Studies in humans have indicated that creatine supplementation does increase PCr levels in muscle cells and that taking creatine for several days beforehand improves athletic performance. But in another study, 30 percent of the subjects either showed no increase in muscle creatine or failed to store enough of it in their muscles to affect their performance.

To have any hopes of performance benefits, creatine supplements have to be taken four to six times a day, an impractical strategy for horses. In a study of Thoroughbred racehorses, creatine supplementation produced no marked increases in muscle creatine and no improvement in performance.

DMG

Dimethylglycine (DMG), a derivative of the amino acid glycine that is found in many foods, also has been proposed to enhance muscles' stores of PCr. Claims of the benefits of DMG supplementation in horses include increased oxygen utilization, reduced lactic acid

accumulation, a strengthened immune system, prevention of tying-up, increased tolerance of vigorous physical activity and improved overall performance.

Some studies suggest that oral supplementation of DMG boosts the human immune system; others show no consistent benefit. DMG's effects on horses have been studied more than most nutraceuticals (but still far from extensively), with mixed results. Studies of DMG supplementation in Standardbreds and Quarter Horses found reduced blood lactate, but a third study in Thoroughbreds found no similar benefits.

Claims that DMG helps reduce the incidence of tying-up are unsubstantiated. Increased lactic acid production (at least as measured in the blood) does not appear to be a feature of this disease, so it's unclear why DMG would have been considered beneficial to horses that tie-up in the first place. The fervor about DMG appears to have died down, and little research has been done on the subject in recent years.

THE BUZZ ON BEE POLLEN

Bee pollen has been heavily promoted as a nutritional super-food. Its nutritional content can vary, depending on the flowers from which it was gathered and the time of the year. It's mostly sugar, with small amounts of protein, fat, water, vitamins and minerals—none large enough to be of conceivable benefit to a horse. Claims that bee pollen enhances performance in humans have been disproved.

HMB

Beta-hydroxy-[b]-methylbutyrate (HMB) is a product made in the muscle tissue from the amino acid leucine. HMB serves as a building block for the production of cholesterol in the muscle, which helps to maintain and rebuild muscle cells. In theory, during stressful situations, such as heavy training and exercise, muscle cells may not be able to manufacture sufficient cholesterol to achieve maximal growth or function; dietary supplementation with HMB would keep blood cholesterol at optimal levels.

Research in humans has indicated that both aerobic performance and muscular strength can be improved with HMB supplementation. Very recent studies in Thoroughbreds also have been promising. One treadmill study found lower muscle-tissue breakdown in HMB-supplemented horses, who also had higher blood glucose levels during exercise than did controls. Another study of racehorses in training and in racing conditions found lower amounts of muscle enzymes (indicative of muscle damage) in those horses whose diets were supplemented with HMB. The racehorses on HMB began racing earlier in the year, had shorter intervals between races and won more races from four weeks into the season until their last races of the year. Initial results of the effects of HMB supplementation are promising, but more work needs to be done.

MSM

Methylsulfonylmethane (MSM) is an odorless and tasteless derivative of the pungent chemical dimethylsulfoxide (DMSO). Its only known action is to supply a readily available source of sulfur to the horse. MSM has been proclaimed to have numerous beneficial effects: moderating allergic reactions and gastrointestinal-tract upset, correcting malabsorption of other nutrients (especially minerals related to developmental orthopedic disease), relieving pain and inflammation and acting as a natural antimicrobial, antioxidant and antiparasitic.

Given orally, MSM appears to end up in every cell as part of organo-sulfur molecules. Still, no scientific evidence exists that dietary MSM is beneficial to horses, and its effectiveness in treating any equine condition is currently mostly anecdotal.

ANTIOXIDANTS

Antioxidants help the horse's body eliminate compounds known as *free radicals*. Free radicals (molecules with unpaired electrons) are very reactive, and those reactions can damage important components of cellular membranes, the nucleic acids that make up cells' genetic code and structural proteins.

Most free radicals are formed while cell *mitochondria* (the cellular organs in which energy is produced) convert oxygen to fuel (in a process known as *oxidation*). During the oxidation process, the oxygen is eventually converted to water; some oxygen molecules, however, escape. Some of these become negatively charged *superoxide anions*, also known as free radicals. A lifetime of damage from oxidative metabolism and free-radical production is believed to decrease the functioning of cellular mitochondria, leading to problems in obtaining sufficient cellular energy and possibly even causing cancer by changing cellular DNA.

Antioxidants protect against free-radical damage by reacting with them; they react with the oxygen radicals before they can do their damage. Vitamins E, C, and beta-carotene are natural antioxidants. Other plant chemicals (phytochemicals) also function as antioxidants and are marketed as such.

Much medical research has been conducted to determine antioxidants' role in preventing disease. Vitamin E appears to be the most beneficial supplement; in horses, it appears to be important in preventing the development of a condition known as equine motor neuron disease. The effects of other types of antioxidants require more investigation.

ORAL JOINT SUPPLEMENTS

Oral joint supplements are said to function as anti-inflammatory agents and/or supply additional building blocks for the formation and maintenance of normal joint cartilage. The goal in their use is to make movement in the joint less painful and to improve joint function.

If you've visited a tack shop lately, you may have noticed that almost two-thirds of the feed-supplement shelves are devoted to these supplements. The products are wonderfully packaged, heavily advertised and impressively endorsed—sometimes even by veterinarians. Still, it's not obvious how or even if they work in horses, nor is it obvious what constitutes a proper dose or how the recommended doses were established.

Most oral joint supplements contain chondroitin sulfate and/or glucosamine, sometimes with various vitamins and minerals added. Chondroitin sulfate is one of the primary building blocks of cartilage. It is found in any tissue that contains cartilage; the most common source fed to horses is the windpipes of cattle. Gluco-samine is a complex sugar molecule from which structural components of normal joint cartilage called *proteoglycans* are made. Almost all foods contain small amounts of glucosamine, and foods that contain cartilage have larger amounts. Crab shells are a common source of the glucosamine that's fed to horses.

Taken orally, chondroitin sulfate *may* have some anti-inflammatory effects in some species. However, at least one study in humans showed that chondroitin sulfate was not absorbed intact from the intestinal tract and concluded that any direct action on joint cartilage is impossible. (Something that's not known is whether the intact molecule or just a portion of it is needed for chondroitin sulfate to be effective.) Due to the size of the chondroitin-sulfate molecule, there is good reason to believe that it *can't* be absorbed. Absorption studies on horses are being conducted, but results haven't yet been published. One thing appears certain, however: Chondroitin sulfate is unlikely to harm your horse.

In one short-term study, oral glucosamine has been shown to be as effective as ibuprofen (a common nonsteroidal anti-inflammatory drug) at controlling the pain and soreness associated with osteoarthritis of the knee in humans. Other studies further indicated that glucosamine has a direct anti-inflammatory effect and that humans absorb it from the gastrointestinal tract.

Can glucosamine help restore damaged joint cartilage or maintain healthy cartilage? Some test-tube evidence suggests that it can, but no research on humans or horses has supported such evidence.

Still, of the array of oral supplements marketed for the treatment of arthritis, glucosamine has shown the most impressive results to date, although no study has looked at any long-term effects.

Only a few research efforts have studied the effects of oral joint supplements on equine joint inflammation. In separate studies, researchers irritated equine knee joints by injecting them with a foreign substance. One group of horses was treated with injections of intravenous hyaluronan, the second with injections of intramuscular polysulfated glycosaminoglycan (PSGAG) and the third with a heavily advertised brand of oral joint supplement. The first two treatments helped relieve the signs of inflammation, with the PSGAG producing the better results of the two; the oral joint supplement had no apparent effect. This study certainly is not the final word on oral joint supplements; it even may not be the best experimental model, because injecting an irritating substance into a joint does not mimic the changes that occur in osteoarthritis. Still, the results of the study showed that the two injectable products helped relieve joint inflammation, but the oral one did not.

Other evaluations of oral joint supplements have been more promising. A pilot study of their effects in an experimentally produced osteoarthritis model showed that the two horses studied experienced clinical relief of lameness, despite the fact that the joint fluid appeared unaffected.

In another study of the effects of an oral joint supplement on twenty-five horses with osteoarthritis, the treated horses showed statistically significant improvement, as measured by a lowered lameness score, decreased response to flexion tests and increased length of stride. Improvement was noted just two weeks after the onset of therapy and continued to the end of the six-week study. A third, recently reported study showed that oral joint supplements produced some improvement in horses affected with navicular syndrome. Although these studies were not published in peer-reviewed journals, they at least suggest that these products warrant further investigation.

If you purchase an oral joint supplement, you get what's on the label, right? According to research at the University of Maryland, that's not necessarily the case. When researchers tested twenty-seven glucosamine or chondroitin sulfate products (the brand names, unfortunately, were not revealed), they found that several did not contain the amounts of the active ingredients that the labels claimed. Furthermore, different batches of the same product can contain different concentrations.

Even if you find a selection of apparently good-quality oral joint supplements from which to choose, you're faced with the dilemma of evaluating the source of the active ingredients. Some products are derived from cattle windpipes; another is made from shark cartilage; yet another comes from mussels (and smells like it, too). Mussels and shark cartilage do not contain glucosamine. At this time, however, the source of the glucosamine and chondroitin sulfate does not appear to affect the product's effectiveness.

BUILD YOUR MUSSELS

An extract from the domestically farmed New Zealand green-lipped mussel (*Perna canaliculus*) is just one more in a long line of non-drug substances marketed as anti-arthritic. Studies in small animals and in humans have failed to produce any evidence that the mussel is effective in this regard, and studies in rats failed to show any anti-inflammatory effect. The extract isn't toxic and doesn't cause significant side effects (unless you're allergic to shellfish), but it doesn't appear to have any therapeutic benefits, either.

So what's the bottom line? Should you give your horse oral joint supplements to help treat or prevent arthritis? No clear answer exists at this time. Research indicates that glucosamine in particular may have some promising anti-inflammatory and joint-protective effects, particularly if used early in the treatment of arthritis.

The supplements won't hurt your horse (your pocketbook is another matter), and many people (including veterinarians) recommend them. But they have not been proven to be consistently effective in relieving inflammation or promoting cartilage health, and they're almost certain not to work in horses with advanced osteoarthritis, because they may not have much cartilage left to restore. Finally, no dosage amounts of these products have been established.

Until some standards of quality and purity are adopted, make sure that any oral joint supplements you purchase are properly labeled, adequately tested and reasonably effective. Meanwhile, don't rely solely on these products to prevent or treat equine joint problems.

IMPLICATIONS FOR HORSE OWNERS

The FDA has taken notice of the claims made by nutraceutical manufacturers and consumer demand for these products. The

January/February 1999 issue of *The FDA Veterinarian* contains the following statement:

> Since [a nutraceutical product] has not undergone the same testing for safety and efficacy as required for approved drugs, it is impossible to know whether the product works at all or is even unsafe . . . Due to the large number of products on the market, it is sometimes difficult for FDA and state regulatory officials to effectively police them all. Therefore, the consumer should eye with scrutiny any claims that a dietary supplement or nutraceutical is useful for the treatment or prevention of disease or promises that it will "improve" a condition or make the pet "healthier." As with any supplement, the pet owner should discuss the use of a product for a pet with his or her veterinarian first.

It should be clear that the claims made for nutraceuticals sold to horse owners have not been adequately tested. Because efficacy and safety testing are not currently required in order to market most such products, it is difficult to say whether such testing will ever be done. You, the consumer, are in the awkward position of having to do the research yourself, with your horse the subject of that research.

KATHLEEN CRANDELL

Dr. Kathleen Crandell holds an M.S. in equine nutrition and exercise physiology and a Ph.D. in equine nutrition and reproduction from Virginia Polytechnic Institute and State University. She is a nutritionist with Kentucky Equine Research, Inc., in Versailles, where she provides consultation and technical support to East Coast and South American clientele.

STEPHEN DUREN

Dr. Stephen Duren holds a B.S. in animal science from the University of Idaho and an M.S. in equine nutrition (focusing on the influence of feeding fat to performance horses) and a Ph.D. in equine nutrition and exercise physiology (focusing on the changes in cardiac output associated with feeding and exercise) from the University of Kentucky. He is a consulting equine nutritionist with Kentucky Equine Research, Inc.

CHAPTER FIFTEEN

Where Do You Go from Here?

with Timothy Gorski, M.D., FADOG

After listening to the claims made for various therapies, you may come away with the impression that the only thing that matters is whether you believe in the therapy in question. After reading the preceding fourteen chapters, you also may have concluded that doctors and veterinarians are skeptical of alternative therapies because they're narrow-minded, egotistical, jealous of reports of alternative practitioners' success, and worried about protecting their turf and their livelihoods. For most veterinarians, this simply isn't the case.

Successful scientists (including doctors and veterinarians) have to be open-minded and creative if they hope to develop new ideas and experiments to test their ideas. In fact, some studies show that scientific researchers are more open-minded than people who promote alternative therapies. But scientists become concerned when they see so many ideas about health and nutrition seriously conflicting with established truths and scientific principles.

It's true that many science-based ideas and methods once thought promising have been discarded. Some such ideas and methods were promoted by researchers who allowed their enthusiasm to override their better judgment. But these false starts and dead ends have motivated most scientists to be on guard against ideas that are unlikely to hold up under scrutiny.

The essence of science is a delicate balancing act. On the one hand, scientists are attracted to strange and exotic ideas because they are eager to be part of discoveries and revolutionary changes. On the other hand, they are wary of being led astray by emotional attachments to their own ideas or even by their own enthusiasm. They know that there are only a few ways to get things right and many ways to be misled. That's where scientific investigations come in. You, the horse owner, can learn to exercise similar caution.

The life and health of your horse may depend on your ability to evaluate objectively whether a recommended treatment is valid or bogus. At best, dabbling in dubious therapeutic methods is a waste of time and money. At worst, it may delay or deny your horse receiving beneficial therapy and prolong her suffering. This chapter has a few guidelines to help you make informed decisions as you wade through the array of treatments and products available in today's marketplace.

CONSULT YOUR VETERINARIAN

Your veterinarian is specially trained in the medical care and treatment of animals. If your vet can't identify or treat your horse's problem, he or she should be able to refer you to other experts who can.

Don't hesitate to get a second or even a third opinion, particularly if you don't understand a diagnosis or a proposed treatment, if what you're told contradicts what you've heard or learned or if the proposed course of action is significantly more expensive than what you expected. Legitimate differences of medical opinion do exist, but an ethical veterinarian will readily acknowledge this fact and will be happy either to discuss other options or to work with other professionals to help you get the best results for your horse.

CHECK CREDENTIALS

Certified therapists are not necessarily recognized veterinary experts, and not all groups with scientific-sounding names are reputable. Do your homework and find out what the certification means. In the United States, licensed veterinarians are either D.V.M.s or V.M.D.s; organizations such as the American College of Veterinary Surgeons, the American College of Veterinary Internal Medicine and several others offer specialty certifications.

If you're considering a practitioner whose main or only source of income is providing a particular therapy, or if he or she stands to profit from the sale of a particular therapeutic product, there is a strong economic incentive for that person to find a reason to use that product, regardless of whether your horse needs it.

Don't rush to pay to make your horse part of an experiment. Most legi-timate scientific research is funded through grants that cover the costs. If you are asked to participate in a study, obtain a copy of the experimental protocol before you sign up.

EXAMINE THE EVIDENCE

Evaluating a therapy's effectiveness can be difficult (as you may have gathered after reading this far), and it's doubly difficult if you're not a scientist or a medical professional. As you consider various therapeutic options, keep in mind that all evidence is not of the same quality and value.

Negative results count more against a claim than positive results count for it—especially if negative results continue to appear as a treatment is studied, even if positive results outnumber the negative ones. The reason is simple: Bona fide positive results should be reproducible by different people under different conditions; but if a treatment works only for certain people under certain conditions, it probably won't work for your horse under its particular circumstances.

Ideas about health and medical care should be easy to test directly. If someone tells you that the flow of your horse's *qi* energy is abnormal, ask the practitioner to demonstrate the abnormality. If you're told that a homeopathic preparation contains an imprint of a molecular vibration, expect that such vibrations are measurable and ask to see supporting data.

Consider, too, whether the body of evidence supporting a therapy or treatment has increased over time. In the 1960s, for example, scientists had only a vague understanding of DNA's role in genetics. Today, molecular biologists can isolate single genes, determine their exact DNA structure and the protein molecules they code for and even clone and transplant them from one organism to another.

190

But what has happened to homeopathy's speculative "Law of Similars" and "Law of Infinitesimals" since they were first described 200 years ago by Samuel Hahnemann? How much more have chiropractors been able to discover about the "spinal subluxations" they have claimed to treat for more than a century? And where is the evidence for *qi* energy after thousands of years? None of these ideas is any better substantiated or understood today than when they were first proposed.

Be even more skeptical about health- and nutrition-related claims if they conflict with well-established facts and principles. If homeopathy is valid, for instance, why does diluting lemonade with water weaken its color and taste instead of strengthening it, as homeopathy's "Law of Infinitesimals" maintains?

OBTAIN A THOROUGH DIAGNOSIS

If you suspect that something is wrong with your horse, collect as much objective evidence as you can. Your feelings and intuition, although they may be of value, also can be wrong; leave as little room for error as possible. The more that subjective assessments are used in evaluation and diagnosis, the greater the likelihood of mistakes. Blood tests and temperature readings are better than clinical impressions; radiographs and ultrasounds are better than the feeling that something's "not right." Get as much objective evidence as is appropriate for each case.

It may be true that the proverbial ounce of prevention is worth a pound of cure. Still, be wary of so-called preventive treatments, especially if they are supposed to prevent complex problems such as colic or arthritis. You can't know in advance which horse is going to develop which problem. Trying to prevent most medical problems through unproven preventive measures is a waste of time and money. Even if a treatment or supplement might have beneficial long-term effects, it could also have cumulative long-term dangers.

CHOOSE TREATMENTS WISELY

Be suspicious of testimonials; proven therapies are rarely promoted this way. When you ask for supporting documentation for the proposed treatment, look for articles from the scientific literature (a veterinary school library can tell you which journals are legitimate and well-respected); newspaper and magazine articles, advertisements, promotional literature, or self-published pamphlets aren't sufficient.

Avoid therapies that have their basis in culture, society, or politics; effective medicine knows no cultural bounds. No ancient, hidden or exotic medical traditions are as good as—let alone superior to—modern medical science. The astonishing improvement in human health and longevity during the twentieth century is entirely the result of evidence-based advancements in public health and hygiene, progress in agriculture and food-handling technology and improved medical and surgical techniques. None of the traditional systems of alternative medical care, which are based on unscientific ideas about health and nutrition, achieved a fraction of this success in all their years of existence.

Beware of therapies that are based on speculation, especially when they involve entities and forces whose existence cannot be shown to exist. Circulating energy fields, vibrations, auras, subluxations, and vital forces have never been demonstrated objectively. If you can't prove they're there, how can you tell whether there's something wrong with them? It has been claimed that ordinary magnetic and electric fields can be manipulated to cure illness, but even these ideas are speculative because they haven't been demonstrated objectively.

Beware, too, of therapies touted as cures for a wide range of unrelated conditions. Most useful therapies are effective for certain conditions and useless for others, which is why an accurate diagnosis of your horse's problem is so important. If a treatment is said to be able to cure or prevent many different things, it is unlikely to be of more than marginal value for anything.

Avoid therapies that claim to be based on secret knowledge, special processes unknown to others or special ingredients that are unavailable elsewhere. Things that work and are known to work are not secrets, and no legitimate medical professional would keep a treatment secret, anyway.

Your skeptical radar should start buzzing if you hear or read about a product or treatment that's promoted as "all natural." The underlying assumption is that natural substances and processes are somehow different than, as well as superior to, "unnatural" chemicals and refined products and methods that only interfere with the body. But every "unnatural" chemical is prepared from materials that originally came from nature, using naturally occurring reactions. Many natural substances, such as arsenic, cyanide, and botulism toxin, are harmful. Just because something is natural is no guarantee that it is either safe or effective for your horse.

Promises of quick, dramatic or miraculous results are suspect as well. Even proven medical methods don't always have the desired effects, much less in a rapid, complete and long-lasting fashion. If someone could prevent or end such common troubling conditions as arthritis, colic or equine protozoal myelitis, he or she should have no problem demonstrating it and thereby earning fame, fortune and the undying gratitude of horse owners and veterinarians everywhere.

No treatment is 100-percent safe and effective. If it is effective, it will have side effects, even if every horse doesn't experience them. If you aren't told or don't understand a treatment's risks, you can't make an informed decision as to whether it's warranted in your horse's case. There is no point in risking harm unless there is a larger likelihood of benefit. If you are told to "keep an open mind" about a novel treatment, do so—but keep your pocketbook closed.

TRANSLATE PSEUDOMEDICAL JARGON

Watch out for "weasel words." For example, *may* can also mean *may not*. Improvements in things such as performance, bloom, coat and well-being are difficult to measure (or even define) and therefore mean very little. If a product is promoted as improving something that can't be measured, be suspicious.

Look out for promises that a product will "detoxify" your horse's body, especially if you're told that her immune or endocrine systems need such treatment. Except for the treatment of drug and alcohol addiction, detoxification theories were abandoned in the 1930s. Likewise, there is no scientific basis for someone's telling you that your horse's chemistry, hormones or metabolism needs to be "balanced," that her "nerve energy" must be released, that she must be "brought in harmony with nature" or that "weaknesses" in various organs need to be corrected. These words and phrases do not refer to any recognized medical concepts or conditions.

FOR MORE INFORMATION

Many sources of information about health, health-care professionals and quackery exist on the Internet. Check out the following Web sites:

- National Council for Reliable Health Information: www.ncahf.org

- NCRHI Veterinary Task Force: www.seanet.com/~vettf/

- Health Care Reality Check: www.hcrc.org

- Quackwatch: www.quackwatch.com

- The Skeptic's Dictionary: http://skeptic.com

IF IT WALKS LIKE A DUCK . . .

Most alternative therapy providers sincerely want to help horses, but con artists do exist. Watch out for the following red flags.

THE PARADIGM DEFENSE

A paradigm is a model, an example or a principle. If a new and controversial idea is said to represent a new paradigm, it's being presented as a different way of looking at or thinking about something. For example, Newtonian physics was a paradigm: a principle that stated that invisible forces act on objects that are independent of the space they move in over a unit of time. But Newtonian physics was unable to account for certain physical phenomena, and Albert Einstein suggested what came to be adopted as the new paradigm: that matter, energy and space-time could be mathematically related to one another, with the speed of light as a constant.

But the notion of paradigms does not apply in considering whether a medical or nutritional method works. A method either works or it doesn't, as evidenced by scientific study. So, if a proponent of a controversial health claim responds to criticisms that the claims lack evidence by referring to a "paradigm shift," get out your hip-waders.

CHALLENGES TO SCIENTIFIC CALLS FOR EVIDENCE

Quacks often say that their ideas are supported by plenty of evidence—just not the kind that reductionist or linear-thinking scientists accept. But scientists do not demand any kind of evidence beyond that which is ordinarily considered factual. If someone tells you that no evidence exists of the sort that scientists consider acceptable, translate that to mean, "No good evidence exists." Claims of any kind are either proven or unproven. Because of the enormous number of speculative ideas about all sorts of things, all claims should be considered unproven until and unless they are verified.

Instead of explanations, promoters of quack theories typically offer excuses for the inadequacy of evidence to support their claims, from, "We cannot get funding for our research," and "Our ideas, if investigated, would put others out of business," to "The established organizations are involved in a conspiracy against us for political reasons." But a person who advances such excuses is essentially admitting that his or her ideas are sheer speculation and unsupported by good evidence of any kind.

MISUSE OF SCIENTIFIC TERMINOLOGY

Many quacks take liberties with scientific terminology in order to lend their ideas a veneer of respectability. In doing so, they tend to favor terms that many people equate with the latest cutting-edge scientific thinking. When words and phrases such as *quantum, the uncertainty principle, entropy, synchronicity* and *chaos theory* are used outside of specific contexts involving mathematics, chemistry and physics, their use usually signifies that the people don't quite know what they are talking about but would like you to think that they do. When such words and phrases are combined in novel ways with other popular ideas—forming expressions such as *quantum psychology, democratic entropy,* or *immuno-synchronicity*—it's an almost sure sign that the speaker has gone out on a limb that is not attached to a tree. Similarly, alternative-medicine proponents often refer to science-based practitioners as *allopaths,* a term that relates to ancient

Greek medical practice and has no relationship to the practice of modern medicine.

Aversion to Criticism

Quacks can be remarkably sensitive or defensive, with a tendency to interpret any criticism of their ideas as personal attacks. No one likes having his or her work criticized, of course; but good scientists know that defending a pet idea is not the same as legitimate scientific inquiry. They realize that honest appraisals of their theories' weaknesses help them make further progress.

Recycling of Data

Quacks make a habit of always offering the same old data. If others remain unconvinced because of various objections or marginal results, good scientists go back and replicate or redesign their experiments in order to—they hope—answer their critics with more and better evidence. If this doesn't happen, one wonders what the problem is.

Persecution Complexes

Quacks sometimes react to criticism of their ideas by casting themselves as misunderstood geniuses. In their minds, they are like Galileo or Lister—good scientists whose revolutionary ideas were ignored, ridiculed and discounted by an arrogant establishment. Of course, revolutionary scientists' ideas ultimately are demonstrated to be true if they are valid.

ORGANIZED PERPETUATION

Sadly, if an unsound idea or method gains followers, it tends to be perpetuated because of people's personal, financial or emotional investments in it. Schools and even licensing boards have been established for those claiming to have the specialized knowledge and skills in question. But if those ideas had any merit, they would quickly have been assimilated into the medical mainstream. Unfortunately, institutions established outside the mainstream tend to fiercely resist change and progress, because such things may threaten those institutions' very existence.

You will always be able to find advocates and skeptics of any type of therapy, but deciding whom to believe doesn't have to be a coin-flip. Ask questions, and don't be satisfied with the answers until you understand them. It may take a lot of work, but it will be well worth it for the sake of your horse's health.

TIMOTHY GORSKI

Dr. Timothy Gorski received his M.D. from the University of Wisconsin. He is a practicing OB/GYN physician in Arlington, Texas and a Fellow of the American College of Gynecology. He is a clinical assistant professor in the Department of OB/GYN at the University of North Texas Health Science Center, a staff member of several hospitals in the Dallas/Fort Worth area and a reviewer for the *Journal of the American Medical Association*. Dr. Gorski, who has written extensively on the subject of health fraud, is president of the Dallas/Fort Worth Area Council Against Health Fraud and serves as board member or advisor to several groups concerned with the scientific integrity of medicine.

199

Afterword

Biological systems break down over time and under stress. In spite of your best and most sincere efforts to prevent that breakdown, things happen, and time is not on your side.

Sadly, there is not a cure for every ailment. Still, tremendous advances are taking place in the fields of equine medicine, surgery and nutrition. Just thirty years ago, for example, colic surgery was a virtual death sentence for a horse. Today, it is a routine procedure from which many horses recover fully. As researchers develop a greater understanding of disease and how to prevent and treat it, horses will continue to benefit.

Even with the advances in veterinary medicine, there are many things that veterinarians do not understand; any number of conditions call for newer and better treatments. But not every treatment proposed to help your horse is a good one. Medical history is filled with promising leads that proved futile. Still, science and treatment cannot advance without the creation and testing of new ideas. But as this process continues, you, the horse owner, need to learn how to distinguish which ideas make sense from which are worthless or unfounded. This even-handed approach is the best alternative.

Advocates of a cautious, scientific, skeptical approach to medicine are at times criticized as being opposed to alternative therapies. It's said that such advocates fear alternative approaches because they're afraid of losing business or of new ideas in general. In truth, however, proponents of basing therapeutic decisions on solid evidence are advocating a win-win situation. If good evidence of an alternative treatment's effectiveness can be established, the treatment won't be alternative any more, and there will exist one more welcome method of helping sick or injured horses. But if the treatment can't be proven effective, veterinarians won't waste their time (and their clients' money) trying to apply it. There's nothing for a scientific-minded or skeptical person to fear, because he or she has nothing to lose.

In broad terms, two groups of people tend to embrace alternative therapies. The first group has been described as the "worried well." These are people whose horses may have no problems at all but who want to prevent anything bad from happening to their horses (or to themselves). They may be tempted to resolve their feelings about their horses' natural deficits or inclinations by trying to fix the perceived problems through the use of some product or technique. They also may be tempted to try to explain away their horses' failings by attributing them to some vague or mysterious physical problem. The "worried well" may feel reassured by a good stallside manner from a caring person. If you fall into this category, though, realize that sympathetic attention to your concerns is not the same as the administration of an effective therapy, nor is sympathetic attention provided only by practitioners of alternative therapies.

The second group that tends to turn to alternative therapies consists of people whose horse's condition is either incurable or undiagnosed. These people may be either consumers or practitioners. If you're faced with such a difficult situation, you'll naturally search for a way out. If your veterinarian (or a succession of veterinarians) can't cure your horse's condition or even diagnose his problem, what are you supposed to do? Give up?

Not necessarily. You have a number of options: You could seek a second (or a third or a fourth) opinion. You could consult with experts in various fields. You could do research on your own by using libraries, the telephone or the Internet.

What may not be the best solution, however, is trying every possible course of action on your horse, just because you've heard of it and you have access to a practitioner. If you're in a difficult situation with a horse now or you've been in one in the past, you know that all sorts of people out there are willing to try to help him. Many of these people are well-meaning; some may be trying to sell you a product or a service. But just because someone has something to sell doesn't mean that you should buy it.

Veterinarians wish they could help all horses, but some horses are beyond help, with diseases too advanced to be cured or with no cure available in the first place. Other horses may not have anything clinically wrong with them, but their owners are unsatisfied with their performance and wish veterinary medicine could do something about it. ("Why doesn't *my* horse jump as well as *her* horse does?") Researchers are working hard to find the causes of and cures for difficult conditions, such as arthritis and equine protozoal myelitis. They are trying to learn how to get tendons to heal faster and stronger and to find the reasons for those hard-to-pinpoint performance problems. The solutions are coming—perhaps more slowly than everyone would like—but they are coming. And they're coming as a result of painstaking scientific research.

So what can you, the horse owner, do? Read. Ask questions. Donate money to research efforts. Insist on obtaining valid proof of effectiveness for the therapies you choose, and don't spend your money on the ones that lack good evidence; those that are lacking will eventually go away. Please don't try every nostrum that comes down the pike, even though you feel driven by concern or desperation. By developing a healthy balance of skepticism and open-mindedness, you can help ensure that researchers eventually find answers to the perplexing questions about horses and their health.

Index

205

J

joint supplements, 180–182, 184
  purity of, 183
jostling, 100. *See also* massage

K

Kirlian photography, 62
knots, in muscle, 102

L

lactic acid, 105
laser therapy, 15, 127, 137–138
  acupuncture, 67, 133
  arthritis, 132
  claims, 137
  history, 125–126
  horses, 134–136
  mechanism of action, 128–129
  pain relief, 132–133
  penetration of, 129
  professional opinions, 133–134
  safety, 136–137
  surgery, 125, 127
  tendons, 131, 135
  wound healing, 130–131
longevity, of therapy, 17, 32, 38
lymphatic fluid, and massage, 104

M

MRI (magnetic resonance imaging), 119
MSM (Methylsulfonyl methane), 178–179
magnetism, 16, 32. *See also* electromagnetism
  alternating poles and, 117
  and blood flow, 118–120, 122
  Faraday's Law, 115–116
  geometry of, 117–118
  Hall Effect, 116, 117
  help or hazard, 114
  history of, 111–113

human imagination, 26
  Mesmer, 57, 111-112, 122
  pain relief, 120–121
  tendons, 115, 121
  unipolar vs. bipolar, 122
  unsupported claims, 123, 193
malaria, 25
manipulation, 83, 84, 85
massage, 104, 110. *See also* backs
  circulation, 102–103
  false claims in, 108–109
  history, 99–100
  injury prevention, 106
  muscle knots, 102
  performance, 107–108
  post-exercise muscle function, 105–106
  relaxation and, 101
  techniques, 100–101
  tissue healing, 106
meridians, 69, 72–73, 75. *See also* qi
Mesmer, Franz Anton, 57, 111–112, 122
meta-analysis, 77, 134, 146
metallic tractors, 112
miasms, 142. *See also* Galen; homeopathy
misdiagnosis, 7–8
mobilization, 84–85, 106
mussels, 183–184
mysticism, 40

N

natural course of disease, 3
natural therapies 28
  harmless, 37, 193
  magnetism, 122
  myth of "natural," 157–158
  "negative" magnetic poles, 118
Newton, Sir Isaac, 56–57, 196
nosodes, 151. *See also* homeopathy
nutraceuticals, 174–183
  definition of, 167, 168
  effectiveness, 171–172